THE WILD HISTORY OF THE AMERICAN WEST

THE GOLD RUSH
TO
CALIFORNIA'S RICHES

David Aretha

MyReportLinks.com Books

an imprint of

Enslow Publishers, Inc.

Box 398, 40 Industrial Road
Berkeley Heights, NJ 07922
USA

MyReportLinks.com Books, an imprint of Enslow Publishers, Inc. MyReportLinks®
is a registered trademark of Enslow Publishers, Inc.

Library of Congress Cataloging-in-Publication Data

Aretha, David.
  The gold rush to California's riches / David Aretha.
      p. cm. — (The wild history of the American West)
  Includes bibliographical references and index.
  ISBN 1-59845-012-3
  1. California—Gold discoveries—Juvenile literature. 2. Gold mines and mining—California—
History—19th century—Juvenile literature. I. Title. II. Series.
  F865.A74 2006
  979.4'03—dc22

                                           2005018611

Printed in the United States of America

10 9 8 7 6 5 4 3 2 1

To Our Readers:
Through the purchase of this book, you and your library gain access to the Report Links that specifically
back up this book.
The Publisher will provide access to the Report Links that back up this book and will keep these Report
Links up to date on **www.myreportlinks.com** for five years from the book's first publication date.
We have done our best to make sure all Internet addresses in this book were active and appropriate when
we went to press. However, the author and the Publisher have no control over, and assume no liability
for, the material available on those Internet sites or on other Web sites they may link to.
The usage of the MyReportLinks.com Books Web site is subject to the terms and conditions stated on the
Usage Policy Statement on **www.myreportlinks.com.**
A password may be required to access the Report Links that back up this book. The password is found
on the bottom of page 4 of this book.
Any comments or suggestions can be sent by e-mail to comments@myreportlinks.com or to the address
on the back cover.

CONTENTS

MyReportLinks.com Books
Great Books, Great Links, Great for Research!

The Internet sites featured in this book can save you hours of research time. These Internet sites—we call them **"Report Links"**—are constantly changing, but we keep them up to date on our Web site.

When you see this "Approved Web Site" logo, you will know that we are directing you to a great Internet site that will help you with your research.

Give it a try! Type http://www.myreportlinks.com into your browser, click on the series title and enter the password, then click on the book title, and scroll down to the Report Links listed for this book.

The Report Links will bring you to great source documents, photographs, and illustrations. MyReportLinks.com Books save you time, feature Report Links that are kept up to date, and make report writing easier than ever! A complete listing of the Report Links can be found on pages 116–117 at the back of the book.

Please see "To Our Readers" on the copyright page for important information about this book, the MyReportLinks.com Web site, and the Report Links that back up this book.

Please enter WGR1719 if asked for a password.

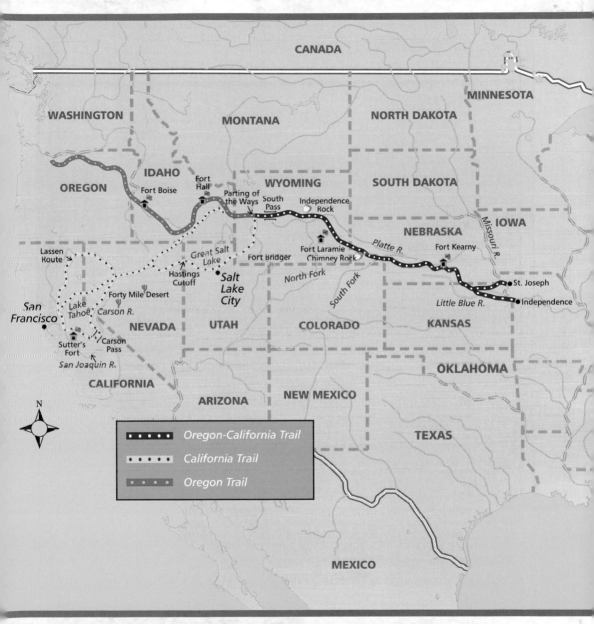

▲ A map of the overland route to California showing the locations of Sutter's Fort and San Francisco.

▷ **1846**—*June:* Americans stage the Bear Flag Revolt and declare California an independent republic.

▷ **1848**—*January 24:* James Marshall discovers gold at John Sutter's sawmill in Coloma, California.

—*January 28:* James Marshall rides to Sutter's Fort to report the discovery of gold to John Sutter. Marshall and Sutter test the gold and verify that it is authentic.

—*January 29:* John Sutter travels to Coloma to see the site where gold was discovered. He asks his workers to keep the gold discovery a secret, but word will soon leak out.

—*March 9:* Miners use a gold rocker for the first time.

—*March 11:* Mormons discover gold on the south fork of the American River.

—*March 15:* The *Californian,* in San Francisco, becomes the first newspaper to print an article about the discovery of gold.

—*March 18:* The *California Star* reports that the nonnative population of San Francisco is 812.

—*May 12:* Storekeeper and *California Star* publisher Samuel Brannan runs through the streets of San Francisco with gold, exclaiming that the American River is filled with the precious metal.

—*May 29:* News of the gold discovery reaches Monterey, at that time California's capital.

—*July 4:* John Bidwell discovers an enormous amount of gold at Bidwell Bar on the Feather River.

—*August:* California Governor Robert B. Mason dispatches Lieutenant Lucien Loeser to Washington, D.C. Loeser carries 230 ounces of gold as evidence of the gold discovery.

—*August 6:* Californians learn that the war between Mexico and the United States has concluded.

—*August 19:* The *New York Herald* runs a story about the gold discovery.

—*November:* The first ship of gold seekers leaves the East Coast for California. The U.S. Post Office opens its first California office.

—*December:* Close to ten thousand people are prospecting around Coloma.

—*December 5:* President James Polk discusses California's gold discovery in a speech to Congress.

▷ **1849**—An estimated one in every five argonauts who journey to California in 1849 die within six months.

—*April:* The first wagon train of gold seekers departs from Missouri and Iowa.

—*October:* The first European gold seekers head for California.

—*October 13:* The California constitution is approved in Monterey. The constitution states that American Indians have no political or legal rights.

—*December 24:* A fire destroys most of San Francisco.

▷ **1849–1850**—Chilean and Mexican miners dominate California's southern mines.

▷ **1850**—The 1850 census states that 92 percent of California's population is male. The Long Tom becomes a popular mining tool.

—*April 13:* The California legislature introduces the foreign miners' tax.

—*September 9:* California is admitted to the Union as a slave-free state.

▷ **1851**—*March 14:* The foreign miners' tax is repealed.

—*August 31:* The clipper ship *Flying Cloud* sails from New York to San Francisco in a record eighty-nine days.

▷ **1853**—Hydraulic mining begins in California.

▷ **1854**—More than three hundred thousand people have made their way to California since the discovery of gold in 1848.

▷ **1855**—The population of San Francisco is now fifty-five thousand.

▷ **1856**—Approximately $465 million worth of gold has been excavated in California since 1848.

▷ **1869**—*May 10:* The Transcontinental Railroad is completed.

▷ **1962**—California surpasses New York to become the most populous state in the nation.

▷ **Present**—An estimated $2 billion worth of gold has been mined in California since 1848.

Having a dog not only provided company, but also helped to guard the miner from predators and claim jumpers.

A BAD CASE OF GOLD FEVER

In 1849, William Swain bid an emotional farewell to his young wife, Sabrina, and their infant daughter. Swain, a loving and devoted husband, wanted more for his family than laborious farm work in Youngstown, New York. So he set out for California, where—according to newspaper accounts—the streams and rivers were laden with gold. Armed with just pans and shovels, the papers said, men were making a fortune. Swain was caught up in gold fever.

Early in 1849, Swain packed his bags and journeyed west, arriving in Independence, Missouri, in April. That was the easy part. From Independence, Swain joined wagon trains of "forty-niners" bound for California. They journeyed over untamed territory. There were no roads, no stores, and no postal service—just hundreds of miles of seemingly endless plains, rugged mountains, wild animals, and American Indians, who were presumed to be dangerous. Back in New York, Sabrina worried about her husband. If she had known how much

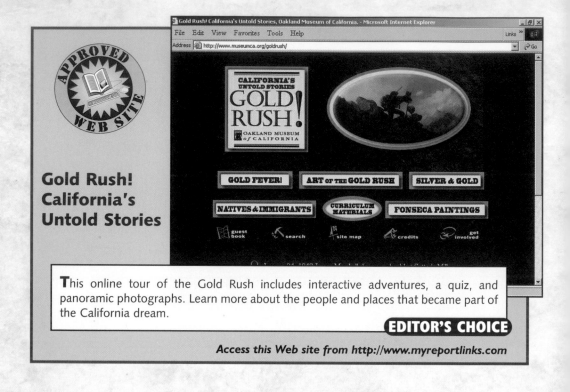

Gold Rush! California's Untold Stories

This online tour of the Gold Rush includes interactive adventures, a quiz, and panoramic photographs. Learn more about the people and places that became part of the California dream.

EDITOR'S CHOICE

Access this Web site from http://www.myreportlinks.com

she would miss him, she wrote to him, she never would have let him go.

Swain's group of "argonauts" (gold seekers) were lucky. Unlike others who would make the trip, no one in their party died from hunger, thirst, or disease (hundreds would die from cholera alone). Nor did they get stranded in the Sierra Nevada Mountains, as had the Donner Party, who resorted to cannibalism to survive.

In July 1849, Swain and his party celebrated their arrival outside Fort Laramie, Wyoming. However, writing to his brother, George, he advised against others making the harrowing journey:

There was some talk between us of your coming to this country. For God's sake think not of it. Stay at home. Tell all whom you know that are thinking of coming that they have to sacrifice everything and face danger in all its forms, for George, thousands have laid and will lay their bones along the routes to and in this country. Tell all that 'death is in the pot' if they attempt to cross the plains and hellish mountains.[1]

During his early days in gold country, Swain described his group as "tired and worn down with toil and exposure but hardy, healthy, and in good spirits, buoyant with hope." Though rain hampered mining in the fall, Swain explained that "occasionally one would make a lucky hit and find his thousands. . . . [T]hose who were lucky

Like William Swain, this old miner appears to be "tired and worn down with toil."

enough to make dams across the streams before the rains often made large sums in a few days and frequently in a few hours."[2]

Swain never found his thousands. Instead, after laboring in the streams day after day, he gathered enough gold dust to buy his necessities. To his frustration, prices in the gold country were sky-high: A frying pan cost six dollars, and a jar of pickles went for eight dollars.

Swain was fortunate enough to share a one-room log cabin with other miners. They stored wooden and tin dishes in the cupboards and large bags of flour under a bed. A fireplace kept them warm in the winter, while the torrent of a nearby stream roared day and night.

When he was not working, sick, or hungry, Swain enjoyed the majestic beauty of central California. He wrote, "The live oak and numerous other mountain evergreens, besides the pine and cedar, green as spring, are loaded with snow near the mountain top and dripping with rain on its side and base. And this is only a specimen of the hills and scenery on all sides of us."[3]

In the early months, Swain toiled with determination. The hard work would be worth it, he wrote, if it meant he could make a better life for his family upon his return to New York. But over time, hardship and lack of success took their toll. Swain began to lose hope.

In a letter to his brother, Swain complained, "This climate in the mines requires a constitution like iron. Often for weeks during the rainy season it is damp, cold, and sunless, and the labor of getting gold is of the most laborious kind. Exposure causes sickness to a great extent, for in most of the mines tents are all the habitation miners have."[4]

A gentle man by nature, Swain was appalled by the atrocities committed against American Indians, "such as killing the squaws and papooses. Such incidents have fallen under my notice that

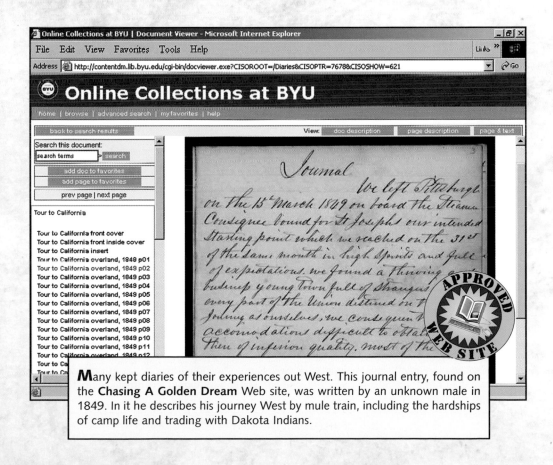

Many kept diaries of their experiences out West. This journal entry, found on the **Chasing A Golden Dream** Web site, was written by an unknown male in 1849. In it he describes his journey West by mule train, including the hardships of camp life and trading with Dakota Indians.

would make humanity weep and men disown their race."[5]

"George," Swain concluded, "I tell you this mining among the mountains is a dog's life. A man has to make a jackass of himself packing loads over mountains that God never designed man to climb, a barbarian by foregoing all the comforts of civilized life, and a heathen by depriving himself of all communication with men away from his immediate circle."[6]

Such an admission made George realize that his brother needed to return to New York. Though William, like the other argonauts, feared returning home a failure, he agreed to George's request. In November 1850, he booked passage on a ship for

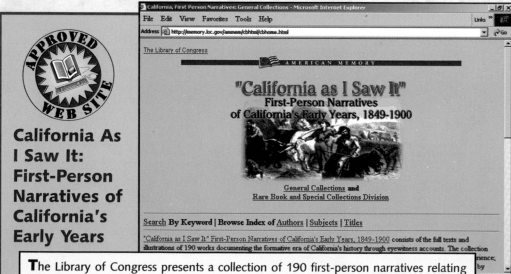

California As I Saw It: First-Person Narratives of California's Early Years

The Library of Congress presents a collection of 190 first-person narratives relating to California's early history, including the Gold Rush. The eyewitness accounts provide detailed information and convey the pioneer spirit that would eventually help to shape the nation.

Access this Web site from http://www.myreportlinks.com

home. After paying for the ticket, he returned with the same amount of money that he had when he left.

Swain returned to his life as a farmer in New York. He and Sabrina had three more children, and he eventually became the biggest peach grower in Niagara County, New York. Surely, he was glad that the hardships of his mining career were over. Yet for the rest of his life, William Swain enjoyed telling his children and grandchildren about his great adventure—partaking in the great California Gold Rush.

Chapter 2

MARSHALL'S GREAT DISCOVERY

When John Sutter of Switzerland arrived in California in 1839, he hoped to make a new life for himself—yet gold was the last thing on his mind. Sutter and his wife and children had left Germany in 1834 because he owed people money. When he arrived in California, which at the time belonged to Mexico, the Mexican government granted him nearly fifty thousand acres of land in the Sacramento Valley, next to the Sierra Nevada Mountains. On that fertile acreage, Sutter hoped to plant vineyards, orchards, and wheat fields and earn enough money to pay off his debts.

At the time, "gold in California" was only the stuff of legend. Back in the 1500s, Spanish invaders had found rich deposits of gold in Mexico and Peru. Spanish explorers hoped to find the treasured metal in California as well, but the dream never materialized. By 1821, Mexico won its independence from Spain and claimed the province of California. Over the next quarter-century, California remained populated by small numbers

http://www.californiahistory.net/chapicslarge/Darlinpaint_6.1.jpg - Microsoft Internet Explorer

File   Edit   View   Favorites   Tools   Help

← Back ▼ → ▼ ⊗ ⬡ ⌂ | ⬡Search ⬡Favorites ⬡Media ⬡ | ⬡▼ ⬡ ⬡ ⬡   Links »

Address ⬡ http://www.californiahistory.net/chapicslarge/Darlinpaint_6.1.jpg   ⬡Go

Gold in California was first discovered by James Wilson Marshall on January 24, 1848, at Sutter's Mill, shown in this painting. This image can be found online at the Web site called **The Gold Rush: California Transformed.**

of Mexican ranchers, American Indians, and American and European settlers, including John Sutter.

One of Sutter's first priorities was building a fort, for he feared hostile encounters from native Mexicans. And indeed, by the mid-1840s tensions between Mexicans and Americans had reached full boil. President James K. Polk wanted to acquire California from Mexico, and so did a party of American landowners and some Mexicans living in California. In June 1846, American settlers living in California staged the Bear Flag Revolt and declared California an independent republic. The Mexican-American War raged from 1846 to 1848, and at its conclusion, a defeated Mexico gave California to the United States.

During the war years, Sutter's settlement flourished. In fact, he needed so much lumber for new construction that he decided to build his own sawmill. He hired carpenter James Marshall to construct the mill. Marshall found the perfect site for the new enterprise: Coloma, about fifty miles northeast of Sutter's Fort. The area included acres of pine trees, just right for lumber, and rested along the American River, whose force would power the sawmill.

▶ Marshall's Great Discovery

In 1847, Marshall and his crew began to dig a tailrace. This was a canal that allowed water to flow from the American River to the sawmill site, where it turned the mill wheel. As the river water flowed through the tailrace, it carried with it sand and small rocks.

On the chilly morning of January 24, 1848, Marshall went to inspect the tailrace. Peering into the water, he noticed something unusual: tiny, shiny particles that appeared to be a precious metal. Recounted Marshall: "I reached my hand down and picked it up; it made my heart thump,

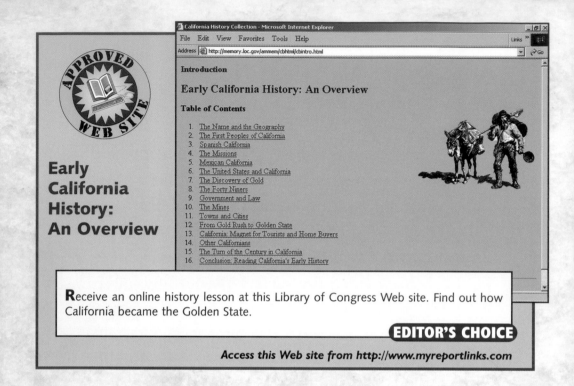

Early California History: An Overview

Receive an online history lesson at this Library of Congress Web site. Find out how California became the Golden State.

EDITOR'S CHOICE

Access this Web site from http://www.myreportlinks.com

for I was certain it was gold. The piece was about half the size and shape of a pea. Then I saw another."[1]

Eager to share his discovery, Marshall raced to the sawmill. "Boys, by God I believe I have found a gold mine!" he shouted to his workers.[2] They, of course, expressed doubt. The glittering pieces were probably fool's gold—yellow iron pyrite of absolutely no value. The men tested a nugget to be sure. The material was compared to a five-dollar gold piece, bitten, and hammered hard. If it were rock, it would have crumbled. Instead, it merely flattened—a characteristic of gold, which is a soft metal.

An excited Marshall felt certain the material was gold, but he wanted to pass it through one more test. After gathering a few more pieces in the river, he took them to Jenny Wimmer, the camp cook. Marshall, knowing that gold could not be damaged by acid or chemicals, had Wimmer place the nuggets in a wash kettle filled with baking soda and lye. When they pulled them out, the pieces were merely cleaner and shinier. There was not a hint of damage.

Sutter Learns of the Find

That week, Marshall made the 50-mile journey on horseback to Sutter's Fort. He arrived in a rainstorm, giddy, telling Sutter that they needed to talk in private. They entered Sutter's office and locked the door. Marshall showed him the precious metal. Consulting the *American Cyclopedia,* the two men ran the material through more tests. They weighed it on a scale against silver, and they dropped it into nitric acid. Sutter was convinced—this was pure gold.

That night, in the rain, Marshall returned to Coloma. Sutter, waiting for the weather to improve, rode his horse to the site several days later. Ironically, the discovery of gold made Sutter uneasy. He envisioned his workers abandoning their jobs in a manic search for gold. Worse, he

This photo of James Marshall was taken sometime around 1872. Years earlier, he had been the first person credited with finding gold in California.

feared his land would be overrun by starry-eyed prospectors.

"The curse of the thing burst upon my mind," Sutter stated. "I saw from the beginning how the end would be, and I had a melancholy ride of it to the sawmill. Of course I knew nothing of the extent of the discovery, but I was satisfied, whether it amounted to much or little, that it would greatly interfere with my plans."[3]

Word Leaks Out

After arriving at the sawmill, Sutter inspected the tailrace. Sure enough, it was littered with gold specks. At the time, neither Sutter nor anyone else owned the land of Coloma according to the local governments. But Sutter felt it was a good idea to buy it quickly. First, he gathered the mill's workers together and asked them to keep the discovery secret until the mill was finished, which they agreed to do. He then negotiated with American Indians to lease the land for three years.

Sutter's next step was to get the United States provisional governor of California, Colonel Robert B. Mason, to confirm the lease. Sutter sent one of his trusted employees, Charles Bennett, to the California capital of Monterey to meet the governor. Bennett took the typical supplies for the 120-mile horseback journey, plus a buckskin sack that contained six ounces of gold flakes. Though he was supposed to conceal the precious treasure, Bennett was not one who could keep a secret.

On his way to Monterey, Bennett stopped at a store in Benicia, where people inquired about the contents of the small sack. Bennett blabbed about the gold. He did the same in a store in Yerba Buena, which later that year would be renamed San Francisco. Soon, the story about gold in Coloma began to spread.

The word leaked at Sutter's Fort, too. When Jacob Wittmer, an employee at the fort, went to the Coloma mill to deliver supplies, Jenny Wimmer paid him in gold. Returning to the fort, Wittmer used the metal to buy brandy. The

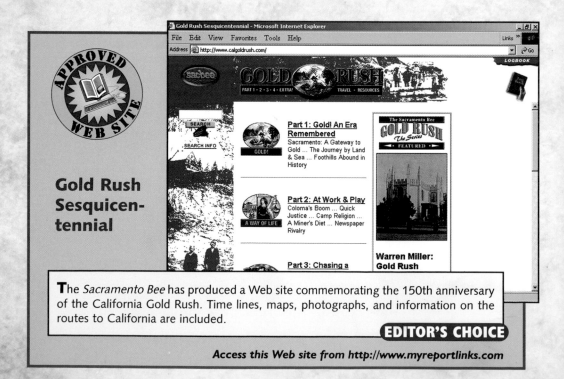

Gold Rush Sesquicen-tennial

The *Sacramento Bee* has produced a Web site commemorating the 150th anniversary of the California Gold Rush. Time lines, maps, photographs, and information on the routes to California are included.

EDITOR'S CHOICE

Access this Web site from http://www.myreportlinks.com

word about the gold spread rapidly throughout the fort.

Coloma, it turned out, was not the only spot for gold. A few miles downstream from the sawmill, Mormon workers employed by Sutter were building a flour mill. After hearing about the Coloma discovery, they explored their own area and found rich deposits of gold. Soon, the news spread about the treasure at Mormon Island.

On March 15, fifty-one days after the initial discovery of gold, the story appeared in a newspaper for the first time. Stated the *Californian*, a newspaper in San Francisco:

> GOLD MINE FOUND: In the newly made race-way of the saw-mill recently erected by Captain Sutter, on the American Fork, gold has been found in considerable quantities. One person brought thirty dollars-worth to New Helvetia, gathered there in a short time. California, no doubt, is rich in mineral wealth, great chances here for scientific capitalists.[4]

Surprisingly, the newspaper's announcement did not cause much of a stir. A month later, however, the editor of another newspaper caught people's attention.

Brannan Trumpets the News

Sam Brannan, a Mormon, had led 238 people of his faith from New York to settle in California. Brannan also was known as a sharp businessman.

▲ A photograph of the area that was once Sutter's Fort, taken in 1866. From this image you can see that the area got congested rather quickly after gold was discovered nearby.

He founded the *California Star* newspaper in San Francisco and operated general stores in San Francisco and Sutter's Fort. Upon hearing the news about the gold, the shrewd entrepreneur got an idea.

For days, Brannan scoured the region to buy every pickax, shovel, and pan that was available. In mid-April, he rode to Coloma and dug up pieces of gold. Still muddy from digging, Brannan returned to San Francisco, waving a bottle full of treasure in the air. "Gold! Gold!" he shouted. "Gold from the American River!"[5]

▶ Seeing is Believing

Brannan's announcement had greater impact than any newspaper story. He stood in the middle of town holding the shiny gold aloft. Townsfolk swarmed around him, eyes wide with excitement. The news rapidly spread throughout the town of San Francisco. Soon, most of the town's population—a few hundred people at the time—left for the foothills of the Sierra Mountains.

Of course, the fortune seekers would need tools to dig for the gold, and that is where Brannan capitalized. He sold metal pans, typically worth just twenty cents, for fifteen dollars. He also sold the pickaxes and shovels for astronomical prices. Within nine weeks, Brannan made thirty-six thousand dollars.

▶ A Scramble to the Gold Fields

So many people headed for the hills that the *Californian* had to suspend publication for lack of readership. In his last issue on May 28, publisher B. R. Buckelew wrote:

> The majority of our subscribers and many of our advertisers have closed their doors and places of business and left town. . . . The whole country, from San Francisco to Los Angeles and from the seashore to the Sierra Nevada, resounds with the sordid cry of "gold! Gold!! GOLD!!!" while the field is left half planted, the house half built, and everything neglected but the manufacture of shovels and pickaxes.[6]

Exploring the California Gold Rush

This online exhibit of Gold Rush history features many relevant documents from the California State Library's extensive manuscript collections. Included are reproductions of original drawings, maps, letters, diaries, cartoons, and more.

EDITOR'S CHOICE

Access this Web site from http://www.myreportlinks.com

News of the gold discovery finally reached the California capital of Monterey on May 29, although people there were skeptical. The alcalde (mayor) of the town, Reverend Walter Colton, sent a messenger to the Coloma area to check if the rumor was true. The messenger returned on June 20, passing out lumps of gold nuggets to an excited crowd.

Wrote Colton:

> The excitement produced was intense; and many were soon busy in their hasty preparations for a departure to the mines. . . . The blacksmith dropped his hammer, the carpenter his plane, the mason his trowel, the farmer his sickle, the baker his loaf, and the tapster his bottle. All were off for the mines, some on horses, some on carts, and some on crutches, and one went in a litter.[7]

▷ Gold Fever Spreads

By July, news about the gold spread to far-off places, including Oregon and Hawaii. Colonel Mason, the provisional governor of California, rode to the Mormon Island diggings. Along the way, he found abandoned houses and mills, with crops left untended. But at Mormon Island, he witnessed two hundred men standing in frigid water panning for flakes of gold. Arriving in Coloma the next day, he saw several thousand miners, digging up approximately forty thousand dollars worth of gold each day.

The gold business was booming. By summer, a dozen stores opened at Sutter's Fort. Charles Weber started a mining company in Tuleburg, which he renamed Stockton. On August 7, Governor Mason announced the end of the Mexican-American War, boosting spirits of white American settlers.

In the summer, news of the gold arrived in Los Angeles, where many American soldiers were stationed. Hundreds of them soon deserted their posts and headed to the mines. After all, they

Johann (John) Augustus Sutter was born in Switzerland and immigrated to the United States to avoid repaying his debts. He moved to California where he built a settlement. Find out more at the **Johann Augustus Sutter 1803–1880** Web site.

learned, miners were making more than fifty times as much per day than soldiers.

Gradually, the news traveled eastward, earning mention in a St. Louis newspaper on August 8. Later in the month, Colonel Mason prepared to send a report and evidence of gold to Washington, D.C. He chose Lieutenant Lucien Loeser to deliver the report and a Chinese tea caddy filled with 230 ounces of gold to the nation's capital. Loeser's journey took many weeks, but he and the gold eventually arrived in Washington.

▶ News Reaches the White House

President Polk, a proponent of western expansionism, trumpeted the news. On December 5, in an address to Congress, Polk declared: "The accounts of the abundance of gold in that territory are of such an extraordinary character as would scarcely command belief were they not corroborated by the authentic reports of officers in the public service."[8]

By December 1848, up to ten thousand people were prospecting around Coloma. Yet, ironically, John Sutter became a victim of the Gold Rush. His employees quit, his land was overrun, and his own attempts at digging gold proved futile. "It was high time to quit this sort of business," he wrote. "The whole expedition proved to be a heavy loss for me."[9]

Sutter's pessimism, however, did not travel back to the east. The New England newspapers reported President Polk's speech. They also published articles that gushed about the riches in "Eldorado," the place of gold. As Christmas approached, optimism filled the air. Businesses in the East prepared to ship tools and supplies to San Francisco, where they would be sold for inflated prices. A winter journey would be nearly impossible, but thousands of men made plans to head west in the spring. The California Gold Rush was about to begin.

TREASURE AND TRAGEDY

During the winter of 1848–49, many Easterners twitched in anticipation. They had heard about the great riches being discovered in California, with newspapers reporting many successes. They themselves were itching to cash in.

"No story of the gold strike was too fantastic to believe," wrote historian Ralph K. Andrist. "Men talked of nuggets to be found by pulling bushes up by the roots, and of streams with beds so paved with gold they reflected a yellow light."[1]

The journey to California would be long, grueling, and expensive, but the adventurous were willing to make the trip. The vast majority of the forty-niners were young men, both single and married. Some were dissatisfied with their jobs as farmers, clerks, or laborers. Others desperately needed money to support their families. Married men typically left behind their wives and children, promising that they would return with a great fortune. Yet in some cases, husbands brought along their wives and kids.

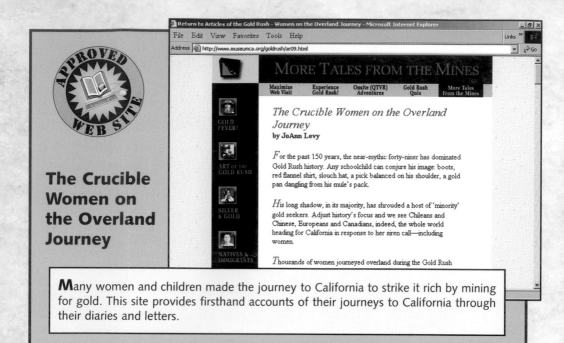

The Crucible Women on the Overland Journey

Return to Articles of the Gold Rush - Women on the Overland Journey - Microsoft Internet Explorer

File   Edit   View   Favorites   Tools   Help   Links »

Address http://www.museumca.org/goldrush/ar09.html   Go

MORE TALES FROM THE MINES

| Maximize Web Visit | Experience Gold Rush! | Onsite (QTVR) Adventures | Gold Rush Quiz | More Tales From the Mines |

GOLD FEVER!

ART OF THE GOLD RUSH

SILVER & GOLD

NATIVES & IMMIGRANTS

The Crucible Women on the Overland Journey
by JoAnn Levy

For the past 150 years, the near-mythic forty-niner has dominated Gold Rush history. Any schoolchild can conjure his image: boots, red flannel shirt, slouch hat, a pick balanced on his shoulder, a gold pan dangling from his mule's pack.

His long shadow, in its majority, has shrouded a host of 'minority' gold seekers. Adjust history's focus and we see Chileans and Chinese, Europeans and Canadians, indeed, the whole world heading for California in response to her siren call—including women.

Thousands of women journeyed overland during the Gold Rush

Many women and children made the journey to California to strike it rich by mining for gold. This site provides firsthand accounts of their journeys to California through their diaries and letters.

Access this Web site from http://www.myreportlinks.com

To pay for their trips, many men borrowed money or were given an advance by an investor, who would share in potential profits. Others sold or pawned their valuable belongings to finance the trip. Eastern businesses catered to the forty-niners' needs, selling everything from boots and shovels to such novelties as gold-washing machines. Other savvy entrepreneurs sold maps, guidebooks, and instruction manuals that explained how to dig for gold.

As the excited adventurers planned their journeys, they sang a rewritten version of "Oh, Susanna." Their spirited song went like this:

I soon shall be in San Francisco
And then I'll look around
And when I see the gold lumps there
I'll pick them off the ground.

Oh, Californi-o,
That's the land for me!
I'm going to Sacramento
With my washbowl on my knee.

▶ Getting to California

Today, one can fly from New York to the West Coast in six hours. But in 1849, getting to California from the East—or even the Midwest—was a monumental challenge. Not only were there no planes or cars, but also railroads did not yet extend to the West, nor did rivers flow in that direction. The Rocky Mountains posed a daunting challenge, as did the desert in the Southwest, and potentially hostile American Indians. Moreover, because the Panama Canal did not yet exist, sea travel took months. Nevertheless, thousands of gold seekers were brave, desperate, and/or foolish enough to make the journey west.

Sailing from the East Coast to California seemed to be the least hazardous route, yet it was incredibly long. Because ships could not "cut through" the Americas, they had to sail south of South America before going north to California. The journey stretched a whopping 17,000 miles.

Nevertheless, thousands of Easterners opted for the all-water route—so much so that they used up all available ships. Seventy ships of New England's whaling fleet were turned over to the passenger business. Even old, abandoned ships were patched together to appease the demanding public.

Travelers paid up to a thousand dollars to journey by sea. The luckiest forty-niners traveled on clipper ships, the fastest vessels on the water. In ideal conditions, a clipper could make the trip in three months. However, other ships, depending on

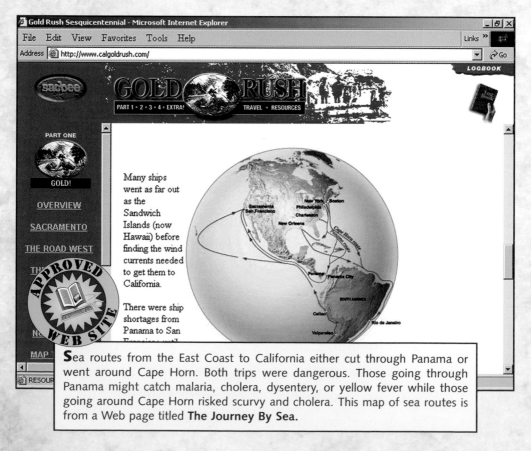

Sea routes from the East Coast to California either cut through Panama or went around Cape Horn. Both trips were dangerous. Those going through Panama might catch malaria, cholera, dysentery, or yellow fever while those going around Cape Horn risked scurvy and cholera. This map of sea routes is from a Web page titled **The Journey By Sea.**

weather and the quality of the vessel, needed four to eight months to reach California.

Though the all-water route was the safest way to go, travelers often endured months of misery. Temperatures could soar to 100°F near the equator and drop to frigid levels off the coast of Brazil. Storms could rip sails and snap masts like twigs. Many ships, especially the patched-together vessels, never completed the journeys. Moreover, many passengers got sick from the weather, spoiled food, or unsanitary conditions. All told, several dozen sea-traveling forty-niners died during their journeys.

Braving the Jungles

Because the Panama Canal was not yet constructed, boats could not pass between Central America and South America. However, gold seekers could sail to Panama, disembark, and brave the Panamanian jungles to reach the Pacific Ocean. From there, another ship would take them to San Francisco. If everything went just right, a traveler could reach California within a few weeks. However, the "gambler's route," as it was called, hardly ever went as planned.

Hiram Pierce, a blacksmith from Troy, New York, left his wife and seven children and set sail for Panama on March 8, 1849. The ship arrived without problems at Chagres, a settlement on the

Caribbean side of the Isthmus of Panama. There, Pierce and his party traveled on a steamboat 17 miles up the Chagres River. They then rode five bongos—flat-bottomed boats propelled by natives—the rest of the way up the river. Pierce was enthralled with the exotic animal life: monkeys, crocodiles, and brightly-colored birds. At one point, the boatmen refused to take their passengers any farther, and did so only when threatened with pistols.

When their river route ended, the travelers rode a mule train driven by natives to the largest city in Panama. They plodded through hot, steamy jungle on a trail that was thick with vines and brush.

Land of Golden Dreams

At this Web site, drawings, manuscripts, letters, broadsides, diaries, and other printed materials and artwork are used to present the history of California's Gold Rush.

Access this Web site from http://www.myreportlinks.com

Pierce counted forty dead mules and horses lying along the route. When Pierce arrived in Panama City, he discovered that two thousand Americans were waiting for a ship to California. Like the others, Pierce waited weeks for a hookup to California. In the process, he became very ill—perhaps from malaria—due to unsanitary conditions.

Pierce's seventy-eight-day ship ride to San Francisco was pure misery. Bad weather tossed passengers about, with the rain ruining the food supply. Sick, starving passengers fought each other for food. "We ketch a piece of meat in the fingers & crowd like a lot of Swine," Pierce wrote. "The ship perhaps so careened that you will have to hold on or stagger and pitch like a Drunken man. Many behave so swineish that I prefer to stay a way unless driven to it by hunger."[2]

In the early 1850s, improvements were made to the Panamanian route. Americans set up hotels along the Isthmus crossing, and more and better ships became available for the Panama-to-San Francisco journey. Nevertheless, the route was always troublesome—and dangerous.

▶ The Overland Journey

Gold seekers who lived in inland states attempted an overland route, usually via wagon trains pulled by oxen or mules. Overland travelers on their way to California—more than twenty thousand of

Once gold was discovered in California, posters such as this one went up luring people to the West.

them in 1849—could choose from several routes. The most popular westward trail started in Iowa and proceeded across several western states. The adventurers had to cross not just the Great Salt Lake Desert in Utah but the Sierra Nevada Mountains in eastern California.

All of the desert treks—be it in Utah or those in the Southwest—were brutal, with many dying of thirst. (Some unscrupulous entrepreneurs ventured to the desert to sell water to the desperate for as much as a hundred dollars a drink!) Moreover, travelers were continuously worried about clashing with American Indians. Sometimes, tribes arrived in force, demanding money for traversing land that they claimed belonged to them. Some hostile American Indians attacked the forty-niners, even though the white men typically carried firearms and were not afraid to use them.

Encounters With Natives

Generally, American Indians were kind to the white people they encountered. "When you read the diaries [of the forty-niners], you find that the American Indians were most helpful," said JoAnn Levy, author of *They Saw the Elephant*. "They sold food, they sold horses, they helped find lost stock. One account is of a chief who took an orphaned child back to St. Louis when her parents died from cholera."[3]

A modern road through the Sierra Nevada Mountains. Back when the forty-niners were making the trek West, they did not have the advantage of modern roadways. The trick was to get across the mountains before the winter weather made them impassable.

Cooking was a challenge to the argonauts, since fresh food was scarce. They typically had to make do on biscuits, coffee, beans, dried beef, and molasses. Lacking wood to make a fire, they often burned dried buffalo dung instead. Moreover, disease ran rampant, with many people dying of cholera, pneumonia, diphtheria, and scurvy. Others were killed by snakebites or trampled to death by oxen.

The overland journey took months to complete. Guides implored travelers to leave in the spring because they needed to reach the Sierra Nevada Mountains before winter. If not, their trek over the mountains surely would be blocked by

"I Am Bound to Stick Awhile Longer:" The California Gold Rush

The University of California at Berkeley offers an annotated bibliography of printed and pictorial materials dating from the Gold Rush days in California. The information is divided into major subject areas such as: the discovery, the journey, Gold Rush women, families, and more.

Access this Web site from http://www.myreportlinks.com

snow—a fate the Donner Party had experienced in the winter of 1846–47.

Seemingly every forty-niner had heard the tragic tale of the Donners. Hoping for a better life in California, the Donners, Reeds, and others— eighty-seven people in all—ventured west in 1846 in twenty-three wagons. The Donner Party suffered great hardships crossing the Wasatch Mountains and the Great Salt Lake Desert. By early November, they were trapped by heavy snow in the Sierra Nevada Mountains. Forty-one of the party members eventually died, with many reluctantly resorting to cannibalism (eating the flesh of the dead) to survive.

For the argonauts, ascending the steep Sierra Nevada Mountains marked the last major challenge on the journey to California. Those who reached the summit, such as Sarah Eleanor Royce, reveled in the paradise below. Wrote Royce in her diary: " . . . I looked, down, far over constantly descending hills, to where a soft haze sent up a warm, rosy glow that seemed to me a smile of welcome . . . I knew I was looking across the Sacramento Valley."[4]

▶ Arriving in California

Getting to the Gold Rush region in the Sierra Nevada foothills and rivers was not easy. The mines were in the middle of California, stretching about two hundred miles from north to south and fully encompassing some twenty thousand square miles. Those who made the overland trip, over the Sierra Nevada Mountains, reached the mines quicker than those who arrived by boat.

Forty-niners who disembarked at San Francisco Bay still had days worth of traveling ahead—mostly via rivers. Sacramento and Stockton were the big cities, but the mining towns were dozens of miles away. Such towns as Murderer's Bar, Whiskey Flat, and Helltown sprang up near various rivers.

http://memory.loc.gov/afc/afccc/p000/p046r.jpg - Microsoft Internet Explorer

File   Edit   View   Favorites   Tools   Help

Links

Address   http://memory.loc.gov/afc/afccc/p000/p046r.jpg

Done

At first, miners used a shallow mining pan to search for California's gold. They mixed water with soil from the riverbed, swirling the mixture in a circular motion. This would wash the soil away and leave the gold behind. This image is part of the Web page, **Today in History: January 24.**

After all of their travels, the forty-niners were typically exhausted. Many were terribly ill, while those who traveled over the plains and desert sported deeply tanned and perhaps burned skin. Yet, upon arrival at the camps, many 'niners felt euphoric. They had completed a great marathon, one that had lasted not a few hours but many months.

When the argonauts arrived in California, especially at the ports of San Francisco, they marvcled at the number of foreign gold seekers in their midst. News of the land's riches had spread worldwide. In late 1849, ships arrived from Hawaii, Great Britain, France, Spain, Portugal, Ireland, Italy, Germany, and Belgium. Others came from Sweden, Chile, Peru, Russia, Mexico, Norway, Tahiti, China, and even Australia. A few hundred of the miners were African Americans. Some were free blacks hoping to improve their lot. Others were slaves, forced to do backbreaking work for their white owners.

Panning for Gold

As the argonauts poured into California in 1849, the number of miners working the goldfields swelled to the tens of thousands. Miners worked in and around rivers, in dense forests, and along rocky hillsides—wherever someone claimed to have found gold. The early-arriving miners generally resented the growing competition, but mostly they focused on their own diggings. Ideally, they hoped to find a mother lode of gold. Practically, they hoped to excavate enough flakes to afford their basic necessities.

In the early months of the Gold Rush, miners needed only a tin pan or an Indian basket to mine for gold. The simple process was called placer mining. Working around the riverbanks, they filled their pans or baskets with gravel or dirt. They added water and swirled it around. Because gold is much heavier than dirt, the dirt would fly out while the gold would sink to the bottom of the pan. That is, if there was any gold.

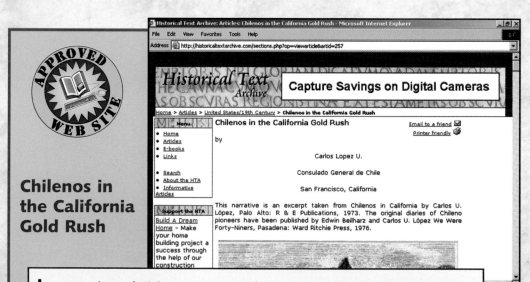

Chilenos in the California Gold Rush

Large numbers of Chileans went to California to mine for gold. They taught later arrivals how to dig and pan for gold. Learn more about their impact on the Gold Rush from this article.

Access this Web site from http://www.myreportlinks.com

Soon the miners scooped up most of the placer gold, and it became clear that they needed more sophisticated mining methods. Miners created some clever inventions, including the gold rocker, Long Tom, and sluice box. Miners ran large loads of soil through these mechanisms, which separated the dirt and gravel from the gold.

Chileans and Mexicans dominated the southern mines in 1849 and 1850. They knew how to separate gold from gravel by using a process called "winnowing." This involved shaking blankets filled with dirt until only gold remained. Yet as they and other miners realized, hard work did not necessarily lead to success.

A Hard, Sad Life

What could be a better job, the argonauts thought, than digging for gold in beautiful California? In realty, mining for the precious metal was a horrific task. Toiling outside all day, workers shivered in the winter and baked in the summer. Many miners worked in the rivers for up to ten hours per day. Even if it was warm outside, the water was frigid since it came from melted snow atop the mountains. Others worked in the mountains, where the terrain was rocky and treacherous. Miners lived in fear of rattlesnakes and their deadly bites.

The argonauts hoped to find large gold nuggets in rivers or rich veins of gold in rock. Yet typically, they found only gold flakes or gold dust. Though they might find a few dollars' worth of gold in a day, their earnings did not buy much. A single egg, for example, could cost as much as three dollars.

In 1849, before towns arose, forty-niners lived in outdoor camps. Some slept in tents or in shacks made of poles and brush. Others slept in caves or under trees. Though they had plenty of "neighbors" to keep them company, miners often were not much for talking. All they could think about

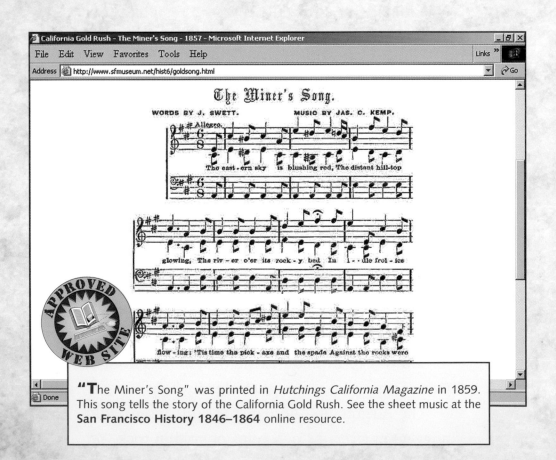

"The Miner's Song" was printed in *Hutchings California Magazine* in 1859. This song tells the story of the California Gold Rush. See the sheet music at the **San Francisco History 1846–1864** online resource.

was their health, their loved ones back home, and finding enough gold to survive.

Ten hours a day of outdoor work was difficult and tedious. Many miners suffered from home-sickness, loneliness, and depression. They did not bother bathing, and their beards grew long and gnarly. Since virtually all of the miners were men, they lacked female companionship. Many looked forward to the arrival of the mail carrier, hoping for a letter from their wife or sweetheart.

The frustration of the miners was expressed in their naming of mining camps: Poverty Hill, Skunk Gulch, and Hell's Delight. Moreover, their ballads reflected loneliness and despair. Many wept to such songs as "The Unhappy Miner," "I Often Think of Writing Home," "I'm Sad and Lonely Here," and "The Miner's Lament."

"The Lousy Miner," written in 1855, summed up the feelings of many. Its final refrain is laced with disappointment:

> Oh, land of gold, you did me deceive,
> And I intend in thee my bones to leave;
> So farewell, home, now my friends grow cold,
> I'm a lousy miner,
> I'm a lousy miner in search of shining gold.

Malnutrition and Disease

Few miners enjoyed a healthy diet. They generally bought food that would keep for a long time, such as beef jerky, canned meat, dried beans, raisins, and flour. Some fished for trout or killed a raccoon for dinner. Many did not eat fresh fruit and vegetables and thus failed to ingest vitamin C. This led to a disease called scurvy. The problems did not end. Those who dug toilet pits too close to rivers polluted their water supplies. Such carelessness could make a whole camp sick.

During the winter or in chilly rain, many gold diggers got wet and sick. Large numbers of men complained of sore muscles and rheumatism. Many suffered from potentially deadly diseases, such as tuberculosis, typhoid, smallpox, and cholera.

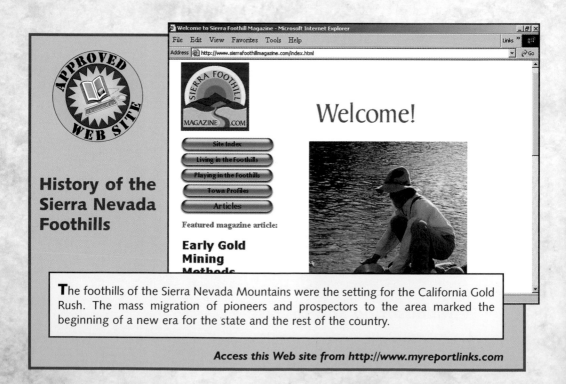

History of the Sierra Nevada Foothills

The foothills of the Sierra Nevada Mountains were the setting for the California Gold Rush. The mass migration of pioneers and prospectors to the area marked the beginning of a new era for the state and the rest of the country.

Access this Web site from http://www.myreportlinks.com

▲ Once miners heard that a fellow prospector had struck it rich, they would stake out claims in nearby locations. This engraving of a mining camp shows a flurry of activity.

In his diary, Hiram Pierce told the story of the walking wounded among him. "Though my back is lame, I appear to be the nearest convalescent [healthy person] of anyone here of our party. Daniel Newcom has a verry sore hand caused by poison. Smith has a sort of felon on his hand caused by rubbing on the cradle, & Haskins hands & feet are sore from Scurvey and Sunburnt."[5]

Miners who became ill knew they were in grave danger. They had no hospitals to go to and often could not find proper shelter. Sadly, the sick were usually treated by phony doctors who sold them fake medicine. Historians claim that one in every five miners who journeyed to California in 1849 died within six months. Yet the tragedy did not end there. Insurance companies would not write policies for forty-niners. Thus, when a miner died, his family was left high and dry.

Success and Failure

For many miners in the Sierra Nevada, the dream of success kept them going. The rivers and mountains were indeed rich with gold. In fact, miners excavated about $60 million a year during the early years of the Gold Rush.

Some of the forty-niners achieved or even exceeded their dreams. One day, Bennager Raspberry pulled his gun's ramrod from the ground. While doing so, he loosened a chunk of

▲ This lonely prospector is depressed after receiving a letter from home. Being so far away from family was heartbreaking for many miners. Sometimes even more heartbreaking was returning home penniless after years of hardship.

quartz rock filled with gold. After digging in the area for three days, Raspberry made seven thousand dollars. In summer 1848, ox-team driver John Sullivan stumbled across a creek brimming with gold dust. His take: twenty-six thousand dollars.

Yet that was a mere pittance compared to the success of brothers John and Daniel Murphy. In Calaveras County in 1848, the Murphys discovered land loaded with the precious metal. By the end of the year, they had amassed a fortune that exceeded a million dollars.

Stoddard's Tale

Throughout the Gold Rush, rumors spread of great mother lodes of gold. Unfortunately for miners, too many of the stories were greatly embellished or simply made up. Thomas Stoddard spun the most infamous tale of all. In 1849, Stoddard limped to a small settlement near Feather River. His foot, he claimed, had been shot with an arrow. Stoddard told intrigued miners that while wandering the hills he had discovered a lake littered with large nuggets of gold. He said he got lost in the mountains and then was attacked by American Indians, who shot him in the foot.

The miners believed every word of Stoddard's tale. A group of twenty-five men even paid him a fee to lead them to "Gold Lake." The onset of cold weather prevented them from venturing into the mountains. By spring 1850, the Stoddard-led expedition, which now numbered nearly a thousand men, began. Yet after a six-day search in the mountains, Stoddard said he could not remember where the lake was. The miners grew angry and threatened to hang Stoddard if he did not find the lake within twenty-four hours. That night, while everyone was sleeping, Stoddard ran away. The gullible miners never found the fabled Gold Lake.

Four years later, however, argonauts discovered a real fortune. At Carson Hill above the Stanislaus River, miners unearthed the largest gold nugget ever found in California. It weighed 195 pounds, and it was valued at $43,534 in the currency of the day. That much gold in 2005 would be worth about $1.2 million. Such discoveries, though rare, buoyed miners' spirits for months.

▶ Giving Up

For most miners, journeying to California had been a big mistake. Yet giving up and heading home was not so easy. Many miners could not afford the ship fares, while others simply were too sick to make a months-long journey. Then there was the matter of pride. Easterners had boasted to their friends that they would strike it rich. They had promised their family that two years of hardship would pay off in a lifetime of wealth. They could not bear the thought of stumbling home as penniless failures.

Many of the men gave up mining and went to towns, asking or even begging for jobs. Others found no reason to live anymore. Historians believe that a thousand miners per year committed suicide. Of course, many miners did swallow their pride. They made the long, sad, arduous journey home, wondering how they would face the loved ones they had disappointed.

BUSINESS IS BOOMING

In the mid-1840s, central California was mostly untamed wilderness. Wolves, coyotes, and grizzly bears rarely saw a human face—or at least a white person's face. But after James Marshall discovered gold in the American River, people swarmed to California. By 1854, the state's population swelled to three hundred thousand. The excavated gold—$450 million worth by 1856—fueled the economy. Popping up everywhere were what the miners called "boomtowns."

▶ Boomtowns

Though miners lived in camps in the early days of the Gold Rush, towns—or boomtowns—began to emerge. Town names were, like the miners them-selves, crude and colorful: Last Chance, Poverty Hill, Rough & Ready, and Fiddletown. Men built not just cabins and houses, but restaurants and hotels as well. Boomtowns featured saloons and gambling halls, where women entertained as singers, dancers, and sometimes prostitutes.

Miners often indulged in vices such as gambling and drinking. Down on their luck with their day jobs, they desperately hoped to strike it rich at the card table. They drank for a variety of reasons: tedium, escape, depression, self-pity. The mix of gambling and booze made the saloons ripe for violence. At any given moment, a fistfight, brawl, or gunfight might erupt.

▲ Many miners passed their leisure time gambling or drinking. Sometimes the gambling helped ease their boredom, or gave them the hope of winning easy cash. Often, however, one night of gambling could wipe out an entire week's pay.

Lawlessness was not limited to the saloons. As more people crowded into the goldfields, and the gold became depleted, tensions in the camps increased. In some camps, a person's claim—the area he was allowed to mine—was only ten square feet. Claim jumping (taking someone else's claim) became a frequent crime. Some swindlers committed the "salting" fraud. They sprinkled a little gold dust on the ground and then sold the land for a lot of money.

Feeling hemmed in, angry, and desperate, many miners committed serious crimes. They robbed and assaulted fellow miners, stole horses, and even committed murder. Miners policed themselves. Camps elected officials to patrol mines and settle disputes. They also developed codes of conduct. In 1853, English miner James M. Hutchings created the "Miner's Ten Commandments," which are summarized as follows:

I. Thou shalt have no other claim than one.

II. Thou shalt not make unto thyself any false claim.

III. Thou shalt not go prospecting before thy claim gives out.

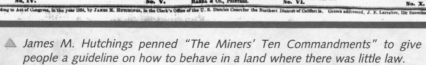

James M. Hutchings penned "The Miners' Ten Commandments" to give people a guideline on how to behave in a land where there was little law.

IV. Thou shalt not remember what thy friends do at home on the Sabbath day, lest the remembrance may not compare favorably with what thou doest here.

V. Though shalt not think more of all thy gold.

VI. Thou shalt not kill.

VII. Thou shalt not grow discouraged.

VIII. Thou shalt not steal a pick, or a shovel, or a pan from thy fellow-miner.

IX. Thou shalt not tell any false tales about "good diggings in the mountains," to thy neighbor.

X. Thou shalt not commit unsuitable matrimony, nor covet "single blessedness;" nor forget absent maidens; nor neglect thy "first love."[1]

In most camps, punishment was harsh but fair. If a crime was committed, miners would assemble a jury, and a judge would oversee the trial. Because no jails existed, convicted criminals were sentenced to physical abuse. Typically, they were whipped multiple times, but some criminals were branded and others had their ears cut off. If a man committed an extremely serious crime, such as murder, he likely was sentenced to death by hanging.

In the crowded camps, crime ran rampant. In the course of twenty-four hours, recalled Dame Shirley, her camp had "twenty-four murders, fearful accidents, bloody deaths, a mob, whippings, a hanging, an attempt at suicide, and a fatal duel."[2]

Many men were hanged during the Gold Rush, but only one woman is known to have suffered such a fate. A Mexican woman named Juanita, who killed a man with a knife, was sentenced to death. Her final words as they wrapped a noose around her neck: "Adios, señores."[3]

Over time, businesses began to flourish, including bakeries, barbershops, and pharmacies.

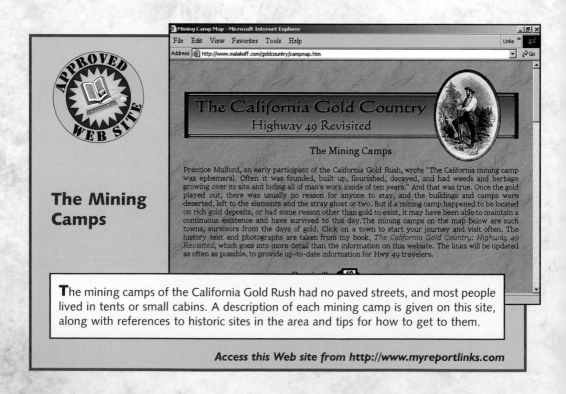

The Mining Camps

The California Gold Country
Highway 49 Revisited

The Mining Camps

Prentice Mulford, an early participant of the California Gold Rush, wrote "The California mining camp was ephemeral. Often it was founded, built up, flourished, decayed, and had weeds and herbage growing over its site and hiding all of man's work inside of ten years." And that was true. Once the gold played out, there was usually no reason for anyone to stay, and the buildings and camps were deserted, left to the elements and the stray ghost or two. But if a mining camp happened to be located on rich gold deposits, or had some reason other than gold to exist, it may have been able to maintain a continuous existence and have survived to this day. The mining camps on the map below are such towns, survivors from the days of gold. Click on a town to start your journey and visit often. The history text and photographs are taken from my book, *The California Gold Country: Highway 49 Revisited*, which goes into more detail than the information on this website. The links will be updated as often as possible, to provide up-to-date information for Hwy 49 travelers.

The mining camps of the California Gold Rush had no paved streets, and most people lived in tents or small cabins. A description of each mining camp is given on this site, along with references to historic sites in the area and tips for how to get to them.

Access this Web site from http://www.myreportlinks.com

General stores offered everything a miner might need in the goldfields, from shovels and axes to pistols and rifles. Customers paid for goods and services with gold. In 1849 an ounce of the precious metal was worth eleven dollars.

By the 1850s, towns became more organized. The establishment of large mining companies, in conjunction with the new small businesses, stabilized the towns. If a man could make a steady living, he might bring his family to live with him. Eventually, people built roads, constructed churches, and erected town halls. As the years passed, life in the Gold Rush region became far more civilized.

Gold Dust Children

The mining towns, where men outnumbered women twenty to one, were no place for children. Poor housing, lack of nutritious foods, rampant diseases, and a violent environment were just some of the reasons to keep kids away. Nevertheless, a fair number of children grew up in the camps.

Schools were not available, so children helped their parents. They might cook, chop wood, or forage in the forest for food. Some kids snuck into saloons, where they joined in the singing and dancing. Money-minded tykes entered saloons and stores after hours. They picked up as many specks of gold they could find. They even used pins to dig gold dust out of the floor cracks.

Some of the children in the camps were orphans whose parent or parents died from disease. The luckiest of these poor souls were cared for by other miners. For some of these men, the orphans took the place of their own children, who waited for their dad's return back East.

▶ Religion

When they were home, argonauts may have gone to church every Sunday. But not in California. Gold became their god, at least in the first couple years of the Rush. In fact, many preachers who had been

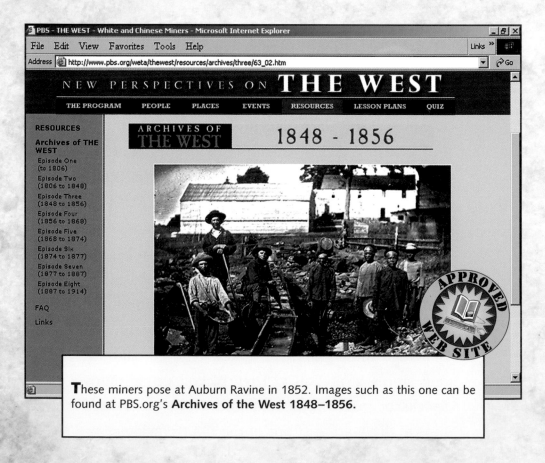

These miners pose at Auburn Ravine in 1852. Images such as this one can be found at PBS.org's **Archives of the West 1848–1856**.

in the region stopped practicing in 1848 and 1849 due to lack of patrons. Some of the "men of cloth" even joined the Gold Rush themselves.

However, as the mania died down and more people settled in the area, religious life returned. Christians constructed churches, while Chinese built temples. Missionaries held services wherever they could find—even above gambling houses. People of many faiths preached and prayed in the Sierra Nevada region: Baptists, Methodists, Presbyterians, Catholics, Episcopalians, and Mormons (members of the Church of Jesus Christ of Latter-day Saints). Chinese were adherents of Confucianism, Taoism, and Buddhism. In 1852, the Temple B'nai Israel was dedicated for those of the Jewish faith.

Organized religion helped bring stability to the Gold Rush region. Towns became more family oriented, and communities grew. More and more, life in California became more civilized. And that attracted even more westbound immigrants.

Statehood and the Rise in Racism

California's population boom, due to its abundance of gold, made it an attractive candidate for statehood. The process was completed quickly. On December 20, 1849, Peter H. Burnett was sworn in as California's first elected governor. On August 13, 1850, a bill for the admission of California passed the U.S. Senate. And on September 9, 1850, California was admitted as the thirty-first state in the union. Boasting 120,000 people at the time, California was nicknamed the "Golden State." Its official motto: "Eureka," which is what miners exclaimed when they discovered gold.

Even though California was admitted as a slave-free state, racism ran rampant. Ironically,

People came from all over the world to seek their fortune in California, such as the Chinese miners depicted in this engraving. Foreign miners, however, were also often the victims of bigotry and racism.

the problem worsened after statehood. White Americans, born in the United States, were officially citizens. But, by United States law, American Indians and foreigners were not. After passage of statehood, white politicians succeeded in passing the Foreign Miners' License Law of 1850. The legislation forced foreigners to pay twenty dollars per month for a license to mine. The law helped whites achieve their goal: to drive out foreigners and American Indians.

Because law enforcement and the courts were comprised of white citizens, white American miners often could get away with abusing foreigners. In San Francisco, white American miners hunted down and killed a group of Frenchmen. In Sonora, whites burned down the town to get rid of the Mexican and Chilean miners who had settled it.

Nonwhites got the message. In 1850, more than fifteen thousand Mexicans and about as many Chileans left California. Fumed Mariano Guadalupe Vallejo, "These legal thieves, clothed in the robes of law, took from us our lands and our houses, and without the least scruple enthroned themselves in our homes like so many powerful kings."[4]

Treatment of American Indians

Whites also were ruthless toward the American Indians who lived near the gold mines. Many

▲ In this engraving by artist J. D. Borthwick, prospectors have created a large wooden flume to divert water from the American River to aid them in their search for golden nuggets.

hundreds of American Indian children were captured and sold into slavery for fifty to two hundred dollars apiece. The California government condoned such action, labeling it an "apprentice" system. Law stated that settlers could keep homeless or jobless American Indians indentured until they were thirty years old.

Whites' treatment of American Indians was nothing short of genocide. Whites burned their homes, destroyed their crops, and murdered entire families. In the first decade of the Gold Rush, up to 100,000 of the 170,000 American Indians living in California had died, according to Dr. Edward Castillo, a Cahuilla Indian who teaches at Sonoma State University. Castillo said that the majority died from violence, while the rest perished from disease and starvation.[5]

New Mining Techniques

As the 1850s progressed, miners realized that the "easy pickings" were gone and that the rivers were "panned out." They needed to dig deeper for gold, and that meant developing sophisticated mining machinery.

Some gold-mining companies concentrated on quartz mining. From mountains or underground, these companies excavated quartz rock that contained veins of gold. Machines, called stamps, crushed the rock, and men separated the rock from the gold.

Over time, miners realized that the richest deposits of gold rested within certain hillsides. Unfortunately, digging tunnels to reach this gold was a massive undertaking. Moreover, no one knew exactly how much gold was inside a hill. Some miners came up with solutions that were more like superstitions. For example, they would wear a gold magnet next to their heart. Supposedly, the magnet would shock them if they walked near a large deposit of gold.

Once miners selected a hill, they began the difficult tunneling process. Using shovels, picks,

Hydraulic gold mining was a popular method of finding gold from the mid-1850s to 1884. While this type of mining did uncover about $100 million worth of gold, it was very damaging to the environment. Learn more about it at the Web page called **Hydraulic Gold Mining in California's Sierra Nevada Mountains.**

and drills, a team of men dug out the dirt and rock. As they moved deep into the hill, they installed wooden support beams in the tunnel to prevent the earth from collapsing. They removed the excavated dirt and rock, which they hoped contained gold.

Many of these miners did, indeed, find large deposits of gold. However, the tunneling process was extremely dangerous. Lanterns near a gas leak could cause an explosion. Moreover, at any moment, the hill could cave in, burying miners alive. Such a scenario was more common when multiple tunnels were dug in the same hill.

One miner recalled an operation involving a 530-foot-long tunnel. Each new foot of digging cost close to a hundred dollars. He concluded: "So you can judge what it costs in money to get into these hill claims to say nothing about the number of lives that are lost by premature explosions and other accidents."[6]

Hydraulic Mining

Aware of the risks of tunneling, a French prospector named Chabot came up with a simpler idea for mining. In 1852, he sprayed the earth with a hose, loosening the dirt. Others quickly improved on his idea. They created extremely powerful hoses by piping down river water from a greater height. In a process called hydraulic mining, men used the hoses to blast huge holes in hillsides. The mud flowed into sluices, which separated the gold from the dirt.

While hydraulic mining was easier for the miners than tunneling, it severely damaged the land. Many hillsides could not handle the constant pummeling. They collapsed, blanketing meadows and farmland with sand and gravel. Thousands of acres of once fertile land were ruined. Moreover, the sediment extracted from the hills filled rivers and streams, causing floods.

Naturalist John Muir was appalled by the effects of hydraulic mining. "The hills have been cut and scalped," he wrote, "and every gorge and gulch and valley torn and disemboweled,

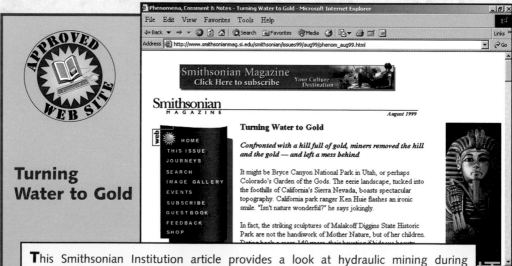

Turning Water to Gold

This Smithsonian Institution article provides a look at hydraulic mining during the California Gold Rush. This method of gold mining used water to uncover rich deposits of the ore but caused rivers to become choked with soil and mud. It also buried rich farmland.

Access this Web site from http://www.myreportlinks.com

expressing a fierce and desperate energy hard to understand."[7]

Conservationists were not the only ones upset about hydraulic mining. Landowners, whose property was ruined by erosion, sued the mining companies. Not until 1892 did Congress appoint a commission to regulate hydraulic mining.

Entrepreneurs

As the 1850s wore on, miners' golden dreams faded away. Those who remained in the gold business worked for large mining companies, earning a modest wage. However, the Gold Rush, for several reasons, greatly inspired entrepreneurship. First, the argonauts were, by nature, adventurers and risk takers. Second, many failed miners, out of desperation, thought up clever ways to make a living. And third, creative business minds thought up new ways to capitalize on the influx of people and wealth in California.

Lucy Stoddard Wakefield was one who seemed desperate. After arriving in California, she divorced her husband. But Wakefield found her niche in a town called Placerville. There she made pies, tons of them, 240 in a week. Charging one dollar per pie, she made a nice living.

Margaret Frink and her husband opened a hotel in Sacramento in 1850. They attracted many customers thanks to a clever gimmick: free, fresh milk to all customers. "This was a great attraction to men," she wrote, "many of whom had not tasted milk for one or two years."[8]

As a young man, Phillip Danforth Armour walked from New York to California. After working unhappily as a ditching contractor, he opened a meat market, carving up hogs and cattle in Placerville. Making good money, Armour moved to Wisconsin and opened a meatpacking plant. His business became Armour & Co., the largest meat packer in the nation.

In 1853 a man in Hangtown, California, offered Indianan John Studebaker a job making wheelbarrows. Prospectors loved the creations

The Gold Rush

Learn about the California Gold Rush from this PBS Web site. Information on the 1848 discovery of gold, the collision of cultures that merged in California, and the impact the discovery had on the American dream are included.

EDITOR'S CHOICE

Access this Web site from http://www.myreportlinks.com

of "Wheelbarrow John." But in 1858, John Studebaker took his eight thousand dollars in savings and returned to South Bend, Indiana. There he established a company that built wagons for westward-bound pioneers and farmers all over the United States. It eventually became the Studebaker automobile company.

Domenico "Domingo" Ghirardelli believed the only thing better than gold was chocolate. Having learned the confectionery trade in Genoa (now part of Italy), he eventually sailed to San Francisco. Ghirardelli failed at mining, so he opened a store in the booming town of Hornitos. Soon he opened another store in Stockton as well as a hotel in San Francisco. Eventually, Ghirardelli built a large factory, from which he shipped chocolate products throughout North America. Even today, Ghirardelli chocolate ranks among the world's finest.

▶ Mailmen

During the Gold Rush, Californians relied on postal carriers to facilitate business transactions and to deliver letters to loved ones. However, the U.S. Postal Service did not open its first California office until November 1848, and its reliability during the 1850s was deemed unacceptable. People instead preferred private delivery companies, called the expresses.

Declared the *Alta California* in 1853: "[The Post Office] has been so useless that business men place no reliance on it, but confide their business entirely to the expresses. In certain interior towns, where the stages arrive and depart daily, an express is as punctual as the sun."[9]

In 1849 failed miner Alexander Todd began his own express company. For delivering a letter, he charged an ounce of gold dust, worth sixteen dollars at the time. Impressed by Todd's success, many other express services sprang up. Some delivered mail from the East, traveling over the rugged mountains.

As new roads were built in California, delivery service improved. In 1856 the U.S. Congress

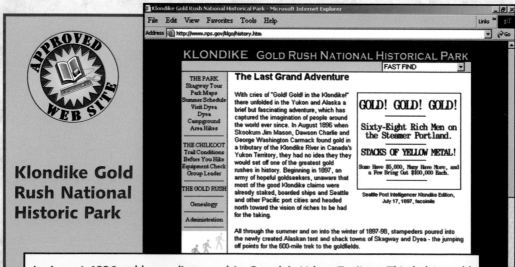

Klondike Gold Rush National Historic Park

In August 1896 gold was discovered in Canada's Yukon Territory. This led to gold seekers traveling north in search of riches. Read about the Klondike Gold Rush from this National Park Service Web site.

Access this Web site from http://www.myreportlinks.com

passed a bill to fund an overland mail service from the East Coast to California. Businessman John Butterfield used a fleet of stagecoaches to deliver mail and freight. Soon, these durable, comfortable Concord stagecoaches carried passengers to the West Coast.

The End of the Rush

By the late 1850s, the California Gold Rush was winding down. Gold was still being mined, but at a slower rate. Though miners produced about $81 million of gold in 1852, they were excavating only about $45 million worth per year in the late 1850s. Moreover, large mining companies dominated the industry. Common folk had to find their fortune elsewhere.

A few lucky ones did, in the territory of Nevada. In 1859, miners Pat McLaughlin and Peter O'Reilly discovered gold at Six-Mile Canyon. Soon, miners unearthed silver in the area, too. Forget California, said the fortune seekers; they packed up their picks and headed east to pursue their dreams.

From 1848 to 1852, California's population had grown from 14,000 to 223,000. But with the Gold Rush winding down, migration to California diminished. Many mining areas became ghost towns, while others evolved into thriving towns and cities.

When the gold mines went barren, mining camps often closed up quickly, leaving abandoned buildings and equipment behind. These became known as ghost towns.

The fates of the forty-niners ran the gamut. Thousands died from illness. Many made a small fortune and returned east to live happily ever after. Others returned home broke and ashamed, hoping to salvage the rest of their lives. Tens of thousands stayed in California. They worked for the mining companies or tried their hand at other occupations. These former argonauts became farmers, factory workers, tailors, bakers, store-keepers, and politicians.

Interestingly, a fair number of forty-niners returned home for only a short while. Having grown accustomed to the adventuresome and "large living" in California, they found their old hometowns dull and boring. Wrote Prentice Mulford: "[T]hey 'staid around' home for a few weeks, turned up their noses at small prices asked for drinks, cigars, and stews, treated everybody, grew restless and were off again."[10]

They went back to California or to pursue another adventure. After experiencing the thrill of the Gold Rush, "living" took on a whole new meaning.

GOLD RUSH LEGENDS

The story of the California Gold Rush is rich with fascinating characters. Some of the legends struck it rich, while others committed dastardly deeds. Some argonauts became famous for their detailed diaries, colorful stories, or singing and dancing routines. These are their stories.

▶ Chroniclers of the Journey

Though publishing methods were primitive in the 1850s, the Gold Rush was well chronicled. Many miners, with no family or friends to talk to, poured their thoughts and emotions into letters. Others, realizing that the Gold Rush was a unique and fascinating event, chronicled their adventures.

Many argonauts wrote about the agony of the journey. Newlywed Catherine Haun recounted her group's travels over the Black Rock Desert:

> The alkali dust of this territory was suffocating, irritating our throats and clouds of it often blinded us. The mirages tantalized us; the water was unfit to drink or to use in any way; animals often perished or were so overcome by heat and exhaustion that they had to be abandoned, or in the case of

▲ *An image of Mrs. John A. Sutter. Tough frontier life hardened many men and women.*

human hunger, the poor jaded creatures were killed and eaten. One of our dogs was so emaciated and exhausted that we were obliged to leave him on this desert and it was said that the [wagon] train following us used him for food.[1]

Luzena Stanley Wilson was a simple woman from Missouri. But she journeyed to California and, as a gifted writer, documented her adventure for future generations. In her memoirs, she recounted what it was like to be one of the few women in the camps:

It was a motley crowd that gathered every day at my table but always at my coming the loud voices were hushed, the swearing ceased, the quarrels

This September 9, 1900, newspaper article from *The Chronicle* provides information on the pioneer women who went to California in the 1830s and 1840s. Read firsthand accounts of their experiences.

Access this Web site from http://www.myreportlinks.com

stopped, and deference and respect were as readily and as heartily tendered me as if I had been a queen. I was a queen. Any woman who had a womanly heart, who spoke a kindly, sympathetic word to the lonely, homesick men, was a queen. . . . Many a miserable unfortunate, stricken down by the horrors of scurvy or Panama fever, died in his lonely, deserted tent, and waited days for the hurrying crowd to bestow the rites of burial. It has been a life-long source of regret to me that I grew hard-hearted like the rest. I was hard-worked, hurried all day, and tired out. . . .[2]

Though she witnessed much suffering and death, Wilson survived and thrived. She cooked and sold food to miners. With her earnings, she built a hotel and a store. When fire wiped out her businesses, she started again in what is now Benicia. Sure, it helped to be lucky in gold country. But Wilson proved that hard work, creative thinking, and perseverance were important, too.

▷ Those Who Struck It Rich

John Charles Frémont paved the way for others to make a westward journey, and he was rewarded with unexpected treasure. A successor to Lewis and Clark, Frémont explored and surveyed much of the American West in the late 1830s and early 1840s. His well-published journals informed readers about California and other territories while captivating them with tales of great adventure.

Many argonauts carried copies of Frémont's journals during their journey west.

In 1847, Frémont bought land in California for three thousand dollars that he thought was on the Pacific shoreline. It was not, yet his blunder made him a fortune. Alex Godey discovered gold in one of Frémont's creeks, and it turned out that his land brimmed with the precious metal. In 1863, Frémont sold his acreage for a reported $6 million—two thousand times what he had paid for it.

John Bidwell's migration to California could not have turned out better. On July 4, 1848, at

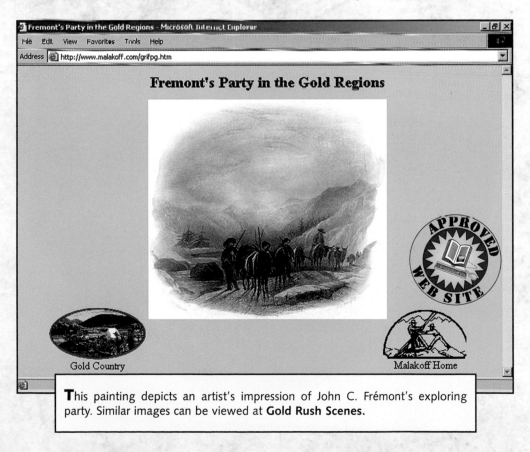

Fremont's Party in the Gold Regions — Microsoft Internet Explorer

File   Edit   View   Favorites   Tools   Help

Address http://www.malakoff.com/grifpg.htm

Fremont's Party in the Gold Regions

APPROVED WEB SITE

Gold Country

Malakoff Home

This painting depicts an artist's impression of John C. Frémont's exploring party. Similar images can be viewed at **Gold Rush Scenes**.

▲ A portrait of John Charles Frémont.

Bidwell Bar on the Feather River, he achieved one of the richest strikes of the Gold Rush. It turned out that Bidwell's land contained a great lode of gold, and he used it to buy thousands of acres of land. Over the years, he became one of the richest and most respected men in California. He served as a United States congressman and even ran for president on the Prohibition ticket. Bidwell's mansion in Chico, California, is now a state park.

James Lick had the best way to get rich: He arrived in California with gold. In January 1848, the native Pennsylvanian sailed to San Francisco with thirty thousand dollars in gold, which he had earned in Peru. Envisioning a thriving

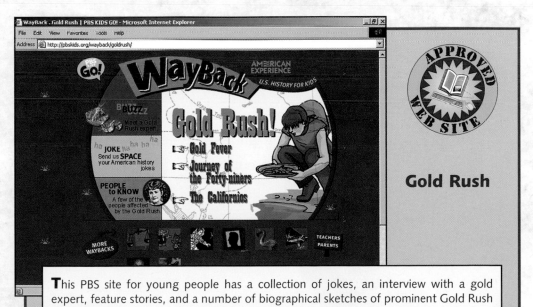

Gold Rush

This PBS site for young people has a collection of jokes, an interview with a gold expert, feature stories, and a number of biographical sketches of prominent Gold Rush characters.

Access this Web site from http://www.myreportlinks.com

society in California, Lick bought thirty-seven lots of land by mid-March. Then, after the discovery of gold, men all over the region sold their property to join the Rush. These men sold enormous amounts of real estate to Lick. As California became more populated, the land became very valuable—and made Lick a millionaire. He had realized what the miners did not: The real fortune was under their own two feet.

▶ The Gold Rush Bandit

In an 1854 novel entitled *The Life and Adventures of Joaquin Murieta,* John Rollin Ridge romanticized the title character. Murieta, he wrote, was a heroic Mexican bandit who sought revenge against American miners who had harmed his family. He was a man of a "generous and noble nature . . . gracefully built and active as a young tiger . . . beloved by all with whom he came in contact."[3]

Joaquin Murieta was a Mexican bandit who is said to have robbed and killed white miners. Although he was a hero in Mexico, he was eventually killed and people would travel for miles to see his severed head.

Joaquin Murieta truly existed, but without the superhero persona. When the foreign miners' tax was imposed in the early 1850s, the real-life Joaquin—like his fellow Mexicans—was forced off his claim. Soon after, groups of Mexican bandits took revenge on those who had forced them from the mines. They stole horses and robbed, assaulted, and killed white miners. According to white law officers, all of the banditos seemed to be named Joaquin, including Joaquin Murieta.

The governor of California offered a thousand dollars for the capture or murder of any bandit named Joaquin. In July 1853, a company of mounted rangers killed a Mexican bandit. They cut off his head and put it in a jar of alcohol for preservation. The rangers claimed their thousand-dollar reward, while the "Head of Joaquin" became a popular side attraction at road shows for years.

The Great Escape Artist

Alexis Orlinski of Poland spent most of the Gold Rush stealing things. From 1850 to 1857, he swiped items including weapons, musical instruments, loads of jewelry, surgical tools, opera glasses, microscopes—even the Holy Bible. He finally was arrested in San Francisco in December 1857, but he did not stay jailed for long. Orlinski busted out of his cell, bonked the guard on the head, stole forty dollars, and left.

▲ Lola Montez was a popular entertainer in the Old West, known for her exotic spider dance.

Arrested again, Orlinski was tossed into the city prison and manacled with heavy chains. On May 21, 1859, he led fellow inmates on an extraordinary escape. They cut through cell wells with a handmade knife. Reaching the prison's blacksmith shop, they used files, hammers, and chisels to remove their chains. From there, they fled into the night. Orlinski was never seen again.

▶ The Entertainers

The hard-living argonauts had thought they had seen it all until dancer Lola Montez arrived in San Francisco in 1853. The beautiful, free-spirited Montez had ignited scandals and even a riot back in Europe. She was married three times and even had a relationship with the king of Bavaria. In California, Montez wowed miners with her exotic "spider dance," which involved shaking rubber tarantulas out of her clothing.

Montez lived two doors down from a six-year-old girl named Lotta Crabtree. Lotta loved to wear Montez's costumes and dance to her German music box. The little red-haired girl, it turned out, was a natural entertainer. With her mother's supervision, she began traveling to all of the mining camps, performing ballads and dancing for the miners. The men showered her with nuggets and coins, which her mother plucked off the floor. Known as "Miss Lotta, the San Francisco Favorite,"

▲ Mark Twain, formerly known as Samuel Clemens, was a popular writer of Western tales. His works are still widely read, studied, and appreciated.

Crabtree eventually took her talents east. She entertained for nearly forty years before enjoying a comfortable retirement.

The Storytellers

Bret Harte and Samuel Clemens wrote about the unusual characters of the Gold Rush era. A reporter and editor, Harte arrived in California in 1854. He wrote one of the most famous stories about life in the goldfields. In "The Luck of Roaring Camp," a baby is born in a wild mining town. The baby, nicknamed "The Luck," changes the behavior of the miners. But fortunes change when a catastrophic flash flood hits the town. "The Luck of Roaring Camp" became world famous, and it helped to further the legend of the California Gold Rush.

Samuel Clemens, by then writing under the pen name Mark Twain, was a complete unknown when he took a job with the *San Francisco Daily Morning Call* in 1864. But after he wrote *The Celebrated Jumping Frog of Calaveras County* in 1865, he shot to national stardom. In this literary classic, Twain describes the escapades of Angels Camp resident Jim Smiley, who bets on anything. Smiley even enters his talented amphibian, Dan'l Webster, in a frog-jumping contest. As with Harte, Twain's colorful tales romanticized the West.

▶ The Hotheaded Editor

In the 1850s, John Nugent served as editor of the *San Francisco Herald*. A master of the English language—and humorous, too—Nugent helped make the *Herald* an influential newspaper. However, he was more than just a pen-pushing intellectual. When someone challenged his opinions, he did not just counter them with an editorial. He challenged them to a duel!

In 1852, Nugent challenged rival newspaper editor Edward Gilbert to a duel, but Gilbert backed down. However, another of Nugent's enemies, politician John Cotter, accepted. On July 15, a large crowd watched Cotter turn and fire a shot into Nugent's thigh. The injury caused Nugent to permanently walk with a limp. Nevertheless, in 1853, Nugent dueled again with another politician, Tom Hayes. After toting rifles for forty paces, Nugent turned and shot wide while Hayes hit Nugent in the arm.

Incredibly enough, Nugent and Hayes went on to become close friends. Such was life in California in the 1850s.

Chapter 6 ▶

THE GOLDEN STATE

After gold was discovered in California in 1848, miners thought up clever ways to make waterways. This flowing water caused erosion, which unearthed gold.

First dozens, then hundreds, then thousands of men worked to create these flows of water. By 1849, they were creating systems of dams and canals. In 1853, they began hydraulic mining. Eventually, about eight thousand miles of waterways ran through the Sierra goldfields.

"We're still in awe today," said Terry Mayfield, water operations manager for the Nevada Irrigation District. "The water system developed by the miners in the early years is absolutely an engineering phenomenon. It's flabbergasting what they accomplished with very few tools and supposedly very little knowledge."[1]

When the forty-niners arrived in California, their sole mission was to get rich from gold. Few did, but in the process they created an extraordinary society. With their hard work, they started

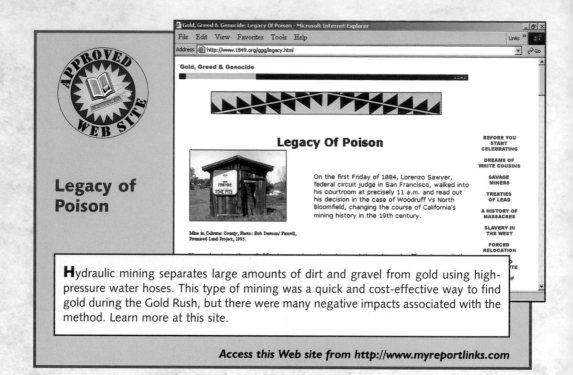

Legacy of Poison

Gold, Greed & Genocide: Legacy Of Poison - Microsoft Internet Explorer

File Edit View Favorites Tools Help   Links

Address http://www.1849.org/ggg/legacy.html   Go

Gold, Greed & Genocide   HOME

Legacy Of Poison

On the first Friday of 1884, Lorenzo Sawyer, federal circuit judge in San Francisco, walked into his courtroom at precisely 11 a.m. and read out his decision in the case of Woodruff Vs North Bloomfield, changing the course of California's mining history in the 19th century.

Mine in Calveras County, Photo: Bob Dawson/ Farwell, Promised Land Project, 1995.

BEFORE YOU
START
CELEBRATING

DREAMS OF
WHITE COUSINS

SAVAGE
MINERS

TREATIES
OF LEAD

A HISTORY OF
MASSACRES

SLAVERY IN
THE WEST

FORCED
RELOCATION

Hydraulic mining separates large amounts of dirt and gravel from gold using high-pressure water hoses. This type of mining was a quick and cost-effective way to find gold during the Gold Rush, but there were many negative impacts associated with the method. Learn more at this site.

Access this Web site from http://www.myreportlinks.com

what would become the most extensive hydraulic network in the country. With their imagination, they created a slew of inventions, from the sluice and rocker to Levi Strauss's blue jeans. By taking risks, they started new businesses all over the region.

The Gold Rush made the world think of California as a land of opportunity. The Rush swelled the state's population and led to its commercial development. Those who made money during the Gold Rush bought farmland, started their own companies, and opened their own stores. California became a giant in the agricultural, shipping, manufacturing, and banking industries.

By 1860, California's population swelled to 380,000, making it the twenty-sixth most populous state. As years passed, the allure of the Golden State attracted more and more new settlers. While foreigners dreamed about America as a land of joy and opportunity, Americans thought the same about California. The state's population swelled to 2.4 million in 1900 and 10.6 million in 1950. In 1962, California surpassed New York to become the most populous state in the nation. By 2003 more than 35 million people called California their home.

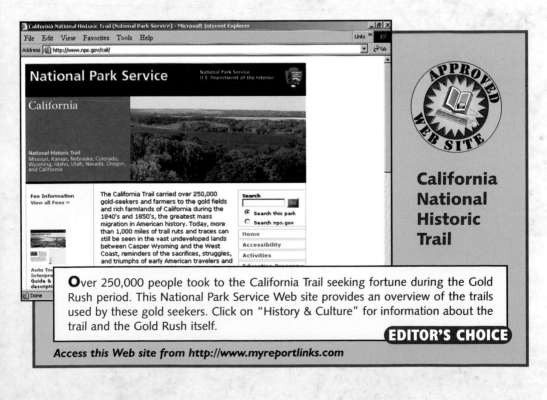

California National Historic Trail

Over 250,000 people took to the California Trail seeking fortune during the Gold Rush period. This National Park Service Web site provides an overview of the trails used by these gold seekers. Click on "History & Culture" for information about the trail and the Gold Rush itself.

EDITOR'S CHOICE

Access this Web site from http://www.myreportlinks.com

A Different Kind of Place

For the most part, the original thirteen colonies were settled by pious folk. Such groups as the Pilgrims and Quakers preferred a simple, quiet existence. They toiled on their farms, prayed, and read the Bible.

However, California's settlers were a much different cast of characters. The typical argonauts had been restless and unsatisfied in their hometowns. They craved money and all the freedom and glamour that came with it. California's settlers were free spirited and adventurous. Explained J. S. Holliday, author of *The World Rushed In:* "The image of California, the spirit, the psyche of

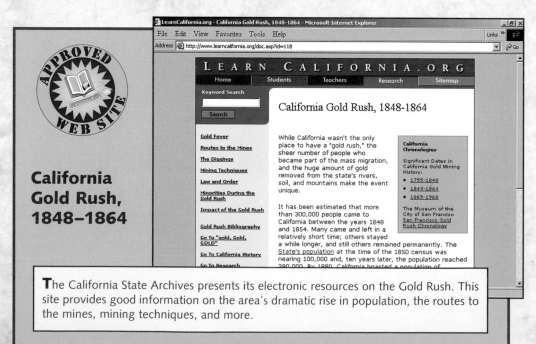

California Gold Rush, 1848–1864

The California State Archives presents its electronic resources on the Gold Rush. This site provides good information on the area's dramatic rise in population, the routes to the mines, mining techniques, and more.

Access this Web site from http://www.myreportlinks.com

California, was shaped by the 49ers—who were vigorous, lustful, energetic, dynamic young men."[2]

Many of the argonauts feared returning home a failure. Yet the vast majority of them did fail in their efforts to get rich. "The result is that people accepted failure," said Holliday, "which is the equivalent of saying they are willing to take risks. And California has been the most risk-taking economy and society in the nation. Maybe in the world."[3]

▲ Many people still come to California seeking fame and fortune as Hollywood stars or celebrities.

Howard Hughes was an aviation pioneer, movie mogul, and wealthy genius. Like many others, he found his riches in California. Sadly, he eventually became a recluse and almost completely withdrew from society.

▷ Modern-Day Fortune Seekers

Ever since the Gold Rush, millions have left their old life to find "treasure" in California. Dreamy-eyed men and women have gone to Hollywood to try to become a star. With an extraordinary collection of talented, chance-taking individuals, Hollywood became a worldwide hub for all forms of popular entertainment: films, television, music, comedy.

In the late 1930s, drought and dust storms made the Plains states unlivable. About two hundred thousand desperados made their way to California, dreaming of lush land for farming. The flood of refugees led to low wages and miserable conditions for most. But some pulled themselves out of poverty and enjoyed fulfilling lives in California.

Howard Hughes's dreams were as big as the forty-niners'. Hughes had inherited a successful drill-bit business from his father in Texas. But young Howard had bigger things in mind. He moved to Hollywood during the Roaring '20s and created the most ambitious movie that had ever been made: the World War I fighter-plane adventure *Hell's Angels*. Hughes also was a trailblazer in aviation. He broke speed records, built the largest airplane ever, and started his own airline. Hughes, like Californians before and since, took chances that consequently benefited mankind.

Starting with the Gold Rush in 1848, the population of San Francisco blossomed, and continues to grow today. People of many different cultures and backgrounds reside in San Francisco.

▶ Sunny Weather

Millions have moved to California because of its warmth and beauty. The Golden State offers wonderfully warm weather, hundreds of beaches, and majestic mountains and forests. The state often is plagued by natural disasters—including earthquakes and wildfires—but people keep on coming. San Diego and San Francisco rank among America's most beautiful major cities. Meanwhile, the beaches surrounding Los Angeles attract bikini-clad sun worshippers.

The 1970s and 1980s saw the emergence of "Silicon Valley," in and around San Jose. Many high-tech companies took root in the area, including Hewlett-Packard and Apple Computer. While large numbers of immigrants lived in poverty in the region, thousands of "techies" got rich. According to writers David Naguib Pellow and Lisa Sun-Hee Park, "The Valley . . . is home to more millionaires per capita than anywhere else in the United States. . . . Homes are bought and sold for millions of dollars each day, yet thousands of fully employed residents live in homeless shelters in San Jose."[4]

A similar living situation is found in the Los Angeles area, as well. While multimillionaires live in enormous mansions in Beverly Hills, thousands struggle for survival in L.A.'s ghettos. Such disparity contributed to major race riots in Los Angeles in 1965 and 1992. Wealth, poverty, racial tension, and violence—they all are situations that resonate with the Gold Rush.

Ethnic Diversity

When word leaked in 1848 about gold in California, fortune seekers from all over the world joined the Rush. Mexicans arrived via horseback. Europeans, South Americans, Australians, and Asians (mostly Chinese) disembarked after long seaward journeys. Many of these groups faced harsh discrimination, but they stayed and took root in California. By the 1850s, San Francisco and mining towns were offering newspapers in various languages.

Ever since, California has become one of the most ethnically diverse regions in the world. Millions of Mexicans have poured into the state, largely because the country shares a border with California. Nearly 4 million Asians—more than a third of the United States of America's Asian population—live in California. Again, a main reason is proximity. California is closer to China, Japan, and all Southeast Asian countries than any other state.

According to the 2000 census, California was the most ethnically diverse of the continental states. The citizenry was 59 percent white, 32 percent Hispanic American, 11 percent Asian, and 7 percent African American. Moreover, 4.7 percent

Throughout California, there are still many references to the Gold Rush. One is the world-renown Golden Gate Bridge.

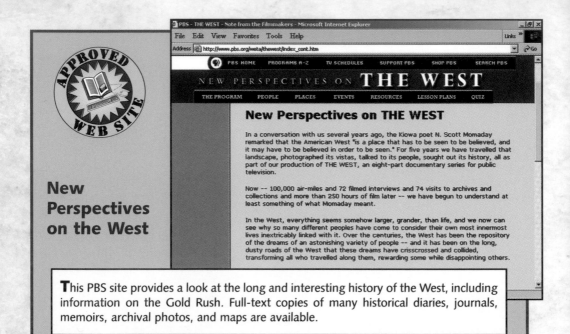

New Perspectives on the West

NEW PERSPECTIVES ON **THE WEST**

New Perspectives on THE WEST

In a conversation with us several years ago, the Kiowa poet N. Scott Momaday remarked that the American West "is a place that has to be seen to be believed, and it may have to be believed in order to be seen." For five years we have travelled that landscape, photographed its vistas, talked to its people, sought out its history, all as part of our production of THE WEST, an eight-part documentary series for public television.

Now -- 100,000 air-miles and 72 filmed interviews and 74 visits to archives and collections and more than 250 hours of film later -- we have begun to understand at least something of what Momaday meant.

In the West, everything seems somehow larger, grander, than life, and we now can see why so many different peoples have come to consider their own most innermost lives inextricably linked with it. Over the centuries, the West has been the repository of the dreams of an astonishing variety of people -- and it has been on the long, dusty roads of the West that these dreams have crisscrossed and collided, transforming all who travelled along them, rewarding some while disappointing others.

This PBS site provides a look at the long and interesting history of the West, including information on the Gold Rush. Full-text copies of many historical diaries, journals, memoirs, archival photos, and maps are available.

Access this Web site from http://www.myreportlinks.com

of Californians listed themselves as multiracial— the highest percentage for any state except Alaska and Hawaii.

On March 18, 1848, the *California Star* reported that the nonnative population of San Francisco was 812: 575 men, 177 women, and 60 children. But this small city was about to get a whole lot bigger. That same month, gold was discovered at Coloma, 135 miles northeast of San Francisco.

San Francisco was the entry port for gold seekers who came via the ocean. Beginning in mid-1849, ships from all over the world sailed into the San Francisco Bay—and they kept on coming. By 1850 the city's population mushroomed to twenty-five thousand. By 1855, it swelled to fifty-five thousand.

Growth of San Francisco

In 1849 and 1850, San Francisco experienced four fires that devastated the city. Moreover, the famed 1906 earthquake killed more than seven hundred people and destroyed twenty-eight thousand buildings. Yet San Francisco bounced back each time. Its importance as a port city ensured its prosperity.

It is estimated that in 2004 San Francisco had a population of over 750,000. Housing costs in the San Francisco Bay area are among the highest in the nation. The reasons: mild weather year-round, gorgeous coastal scenery, and cosmopolitan sophistication. The city's Chinatown is home to one hundred thousand Chinese, who trace their roots to the Gold Rush immigration.

The city has long celebrated its connection to the Rush. The magnificent suspension bridge over San Francisco Bay, which opened in 1937, was dubbed the Golden Gate Bridge. And when the city fielded a professional football team beginning in 1946, they called the new club the San Francisco 49ers.

Sacramento

In 1849, a town emerged along the Sacramento River, called Sacramento. During the Gold Rush,

Sacramento was the prime trading center for miners. Moreover, it became the ultimate destination for many of those headed west—via the wagon trains, riverboats, or, later the Transcontinental Railroad.

In 1850, Sacramento overcame a cholera plague, flooding, and fires. A devastating flood in 1852 virtually wiped out the city. Yet Sacramento recovered, thanks in part to an ambitious project that raised the city above the flood line. In 1854, Sacramento became California's capital. Today, Sacramento is home to more than four hundred thousand residents and often is cited as one of America's "most livable" cities.

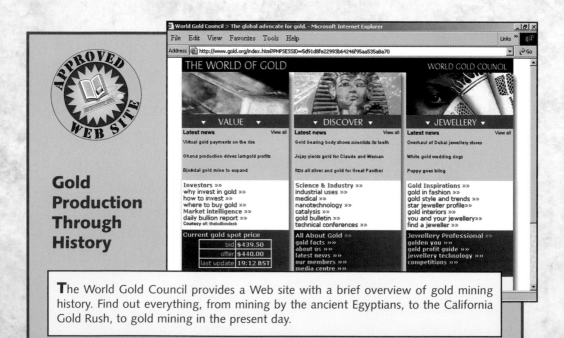

Gold Production Through History

The World Gold Council provides a Web site with a brief overview of gold mining history. Find out everything, from mining by the ancient Egyptians, to the California Gold Rush, to gold mining in the present day.

Access this Web site from http://www.myreportlinks.com

Changing the Nation

Had the Gold Rush attracted just a few thousand people, it would have gone down as an interesting footnote in American history. But the Rush attracted hundreds of thousands of settlers. It changed not just the West Coast but the entire United States. Wrote William Weber Johnson in *The Forty-Niners:* "One thing [the forty-niner] had done, quite by accident but with dizzying speed, was to expand the physical scope of the United States so that it now embraced the entire width of the continent."[5]

With hundreds of thousands of residents, California needed to be better connected to the East. Months-long journeys via wagon trains were not going to cut it. Comfortable stagecoaches were an improvement, but not good enough. In 1862, Congress passed the Pacific Railroad Bill, which allocated funds to companies to build a transcontinental railroad. The dream, which was realized in 1869, has been called the greatest engineering achievement of the nineteenth century. Fittingly, many failed gold seekers, including thousands of Chinese laborers, worked to build the railroads.

The railroads made western expansion easier— not just to California, but to the Midwest, Southwest, and Northwest. Sure, such expansion would have happened eventually, but the Gold Rush sped up the process by years.

Some scholars declare that the Gold Rush made America a more risk-taking country. It sparked Americans to explore new frontiers, take more chances—to go for the gold.

"The California Gold Rush made America a more restless nation—changed the people's sense of their future, their expectations and their values," wrote J. S. Holliday. "Suddenly there was a place to go where everyone could expect to make money quickly; where life could be freer; where one could escape the restraints and conventions and the plodding sameness of life in the Eastern states."[6]

Some say that the Las Vegas casinos are the modern equivalent of the Gold Rush. It is a place where one can make a fortune with one lucky spin at the roulette table. But for those with a romantic bent for the Old West, nothing tops the dream of finding pure gold in the rivers of the Sierra Nevada.

The Modern Forty-Niners

The Gold Rush may have died down by 1860, but gold still remained in California's rivers, hills, and mountains. In fact, since 1848 an estimated $2 billion worth of gold has been mined in the Golden State. Most of it has been excavated by large mining companies. However, individuals still brave the cold river waters in search of golden treasure.

Sure, the gold is scant and hard to find, but it is out there if a person is persistent. Using such gadgetry as metal detectors, modern prospectors can find what the forty-niners could not. For thousands of people, gold mining is a serious—and exhilarating—hobby.

"It's kind of like euphoria," Chris Stathos said of finding a strike. "Your blood starts to run. You can feel your pulse quicken. I don't know if I've broken out into a sweat yet, but I've seen people with gold fever get light-headed and dizzy."[7]

Nearly 160 years later, the spirit of the Gold Rush lives on.

The Internet sites described below can be accessed at http://www.myreportlinks.com

▶**The Gold Rush**
Editor's Choice This PBS guide to the California Gold Rush is a comprehensive source.

▶**Gold Rush! California's Untold Stories**
Editor's Choice The Oakland Museum of California's Gold Rush site includes a virtual tour.

▶**Gold Rush Sesquicentennial**
Editor's Choice Celebrating 150 years of gold mining in California.

▶**California National Historic Trail**
Editor's Choice Many people followed the California Trail in search of fortune.

▶**Exploring the California Gold Rush**
Editor's Choice Learn about California's Gold Rush by examining original documents.

▶**Early California History: An Overview**
Editor's Choice A good overview of early California history.

▶**Archives of the West 1848–1856**
View primary source documents from the Gold Rush era.

▶**California As I Saw It: First-Person Narratives of California's Early Years, 1849–1900**
Full-text primary resources from those who lived and worked during the Gold Rush.

▶**California Gold Rush, 1848–1864**
The Gold Rush was a defining event in California's history.

▶**Chasing A Golden Dream: The Story of the California Trail**
Brigham Young University's library presents this introduction to the historic Gold Rush trails.

▶**Chilenos in the California Gold Rush**
News of gold in California hit Chile in 1848.

▶**The Crucible Women on the Overland Journey**
The women of the California Gold Rush tell their stories.

▶**The Foremothers Tell of Olden Times**
Read Gold Rush stories of women pioneers.

▶**Gold Production Through History**
Learn about the history of gold mining.

▶**Gold Rush**
Read about some of the events and people who shaped California during the Gold Rush.

Report Links

The Internet sites described below can be accessed at
http://www.myreportlinks.com

▶**The Gold Rush: California Transformed**

Learn about the Gold Rush from the California Historical Society.

▶**Gold Rush Scenes**

View images of California during the early years of the Gold Rush.

▶**History of the Sierra Nevada Foothills**

Learn more about the foothills of the Sierra Nevada Mountains.

▶**Hydraulic Gold Mining in California's Sierra Nevada Mountains**

Read a short history of hydraulic mining during California's Gold Rush years.

▶**"I Am Bound to Stick Awhile Longer:" The California Gold Rush Experience**

Experience the California Gold Rush through firsthand accounts and primary documents.

▶**Johann Augustus Sutter 1803–1880**

Read about John Sutter, who lost his fortune when gold was discovered.

▶**The Journey By Sea**

Taking the ocean voyage to gold in California.

▶**Klondike Gold Rush National Historic Park**

Gold was found in Alaska and the Yukon Territory of Canada in 1896.

▶**Land of Golden Dreams**

This historic digital collection brings the Gold Rush to life for you.

▶**Legacy of Poison**

Hydraulic mining was used to find gold during the Gold Rush.

▶**The Mining Camps**

This is a fast-loading and informative clickable map of the "Highway 49" mining camps.

▶**New Perspectives on the West**

A chronicle of the American West.

▶**San Francisco History 1846–1864**

The Virtual Museum of the City of San Francisco presents an exhibit on the Gold Rush.

▶**Today in History: January 24**

The discovery of gold on January 24, 1848 changed life in California forever.

▶**Turning Water to Gold**

A cheap way of mining gold had unforeseen environmental consequences.

argonauts—Those who traveled to California in search of gold. (Originally in Greek mythology: those who sailed with Jason in search of the Golden Fleece.)

claim—A section of land that was staked out, or claimed, by a miner for working.

claim jumping—The act of mining someone else's claim, which was against the rules.

cholera—An intestinal infection caused by the ingestion of contaminated food or water.

Eldorado—A Spanish word for a mythical "City of Gold." During the Gold Rush, people referred to the goldfields of California as Eldorado.

eureka—An exclamation of joy that miners shouted when they found gold.

fool's gold—An iron pyrite that looks like gold but is not.

forty-niners—Those who journeyed to California's gold country in 1849 hoping to strike it rich.

hydraulic mining—The process of using high-pressure hoses to blast hillsides. Mud containing gold flowed down into sluice boxes.

lode—An underground vein of ore that bore gold.

Long Tom—A long rocker with riffles on the bottom that separated gold from sand and gravel.

mother lode—California's principal gold quartz belt, which stretched 120 miles.

nugget—A chunk of gold, usually about the size of a pebble.

panning—A simple mining method. The miner scooped gravel from a creek, stream, or river with a pan and swished it around. Lighter materials spilled over the side of the pan while heavier, gold-bearing particles settled to the bottom.

placer mining—The process of extracting gold from gravel.

prospector—One who examined the land in search of gold.

quartz mining—The labor-intensive process of digging deep underground to find rich deposits of gold.

riffle—Block or rail that is used for sifting and catching gold.

rocker—A wooden box set on rockers used in mining. The rocking motion caused mud to flow through the box, while larger particles—including.

gold—were trapped by riffles on the bottom.

sluice box—A device in which gold-bearing particles were caught by riffles or slats as water flowed through it.

stamp—A mechanical device that smashed ore so that gold could be extracted.

tailrace—A water channel that supplied the force necessary to turn a waterwheel for powering a mill.

vein—A route followed by gold from the lower depths of the earth toward the surface.

Chapter 1. A Bad Case of Gold Fever

1. William Swain as printed in J. S. Holliday, *The World Rushed In* (New York: Simon and Schuster, 1981), p. 319.

2. Ibid., pp. 312–313.

3. Ibid., p. 315.

4. Ibid., p. 328.

5. Ibid.

6. Ibid., p. 317.

Chapter 2. Marshall's Great Discovery

1. James Marshall, as reposted by Steven Boettcher and Michael Trinklein, "Discovery," *The Gold Rush,* 1997, <http://www.pbs.org/goldrush/index.html> (October 2, 2005).

2. Steven Lavoie, "Wimmer's Nugget," *Oakland Museum of California,* 1998, <http://www.museumca.org/goldrush/ar08.html> (January 21, 2005).

3. William Weber Johnson, *The Forty-Niners* (Alexandria, Va.: Time-Life Books, 1974), p. 26.

4. Elliot H. Koeppel, "Introduction," *The California Gold Country: Highway 49 Revisited,* 2000, <http://malakoff.com/goldcountry/tcgcintr.htm> (October 2, 2005).

5. Jad Adkins, "A Metal Far From Base," *Smithonian Magazine,* July 1998, <http://www.smithsonianmag.com/smithsonian/issues98/jul98/object_jul98.html> (January 28, 2005).

6. Koeppel, "Introduction."

7. NORCAL-L Archives, *RootsWeb.com,* February 9, 1999, <http://archiver.rootsweb.com/th/read/NORCAL/1999-02/0918582223> (January 30, 2005).

8. "Gold Fever," *Learn California.org,* n.d., <http://www.learncalifornia.org/doc.asp?id=1928&pagetype=content> (April 9, 2005).

9. Richard Dillon, *Fool's Gold* (Santa Cruz, Calif.: Western Tanager, 1981), p. 296.

Chapter 3. Treasure and Tragedy

1. Ralph K. Andrist, *The California Gold Rush* (New York: American Heritage Publishing Co., Inc., 1961), p. 37.

2. Ibid., p. 41.

3. Steven Boettcher and Michael Trinklein, *"The Journey,"* The Gold Rush, 1997, <http://www.pbs.org/goldrush/journey.html> (October 2, 2005).

4. Sarah Eleanor Royce, *A Frontier Lady* (New Haven, Conn.: Yale University Press, 1932), p. 3.

5. Andrist, p. 72.

Chapter 4. Business Is Booming

1. "The Miner's Ten Commandments," *The Virtual Museum of the City of San Francisco,* n.d., <http://www.sfmuseum.org/hist7/tencom.html> (March 6, 2005).

2. Liza Ketchum, *The Gold Rush* (Boston: Little, Brown and Co., 1996), p. 68.

3. Ralph K. Andrist, *The California Gold Rush* (New York: American Heritage Publishing Co., Inc., 1961), p. 120.

4. Ketchum, p. 96.

5. Stephen Magagnini, "Indians' misfortune was stamped in gold," *Gold Rush,* January 18, 1998, <http://www.calgoldrush.com/part3/03native.html> (March 31, 2005).

6. Malcolm J. Rohrbough, *Days of Gold* (Berkeley, Calif.: University of California Press, 1998), p. 268.

7. Eric Brace, "Mother Lode Memories," *UNo MAS Magazine,* n.d., <http://www.unomas.com/features/motherlode.html> (March 10, 2005).

8. Steve Wiegand, "The California Gold Rush: An era remembered," *Gold Rush,* January 18, 1998, <http://www.calgoldrush.com/part1/01overview.html> (March 10, 2005).

9. Carl Watner, "Plunderers of the Public Revenue," *voluntaryist.com,* October 1995, <http://www.voluntaryist.com/articles/076.php> (March 10, 2005).

10. Rohrbough, pp. 276–277.

Chapter 5. Gold Rush Legends

1. JoAnn Levy, "The Crucible Women on the Overland Journey," *Oakland Museum of California,* 1998, <http://www.museumca.org/goldrush/ar09.html> (March 14, 2005).

2. Luzena Stanley Wilson, "Luzena Stanley Wilson '49er," *New Perspectives on the West,* 2001, <http://www.pbs.org/weta/thewest/resources/archives/three/luzena.htm> (March 15, 2005).

3. Elliot H. Koeppel, "Joaquin Murieta," *The California Gold Country: Highway 49 Revisited,* 2000, <http://malakoff.com/grpjomu.htm> (March 16, 2005).

Chapter 6. The Golden State

1. Nancy Vogel, "Miners learned tricks to slake a state's thirst," *Gold Rush,* January 18, 1998, <http://www.calgoldrush.com/part4/04water.html> (March 20, 2005).

2. Steven Boettcher and Michael Trinklein, "Impact," *The Gold Rush,* 1997, <http://www.pbs.org/goldrush/impact.html> (October 2, 2005).

3. Ibid.

4. David Naguib Pellow and Lisa Sun-Hee Park, "Silicon Valley," from their book *The Silicon Valley of Dreams: Environmental Injustice, Immigrant Workers, and the High-Tech Global Economy,* 2003, as reposted on Wikipedia, September 26, 2005, <http://en.wikipedia.org/wiki/Silicon_Valley> (October 2, 2005).

5. William Weber Johnson, *The Forty-Niners* (Alexandria, Va.: *Time-Life Books,* 1974), p. 207.

6. Steve Wiegand, "The California Gold Rush: An era remembered," *Gold Rush,* January 18, 1998, <http://www.calgoldrush.com/part1/01overview.html> (March 24, 2005).

7. Mareva Brown, "Prospectors still prowl the hills in gold fever's grip," *Gold Rush,* January 18, 1998, <http://www.calgoldrush.com/part4/04modern.html> (March 24, 2005).

Altman, Linda Jacobs. *The California Gold Rush in American History*. Springfield, N.J.: Enslow Publishers, Inc., 1997.

Blashfield, Jean F. *The California Gold Rush*. Minneapolis: Compass Point Books, 2001.

Dolan, Edward F. *The California Gold Rush*. New York: Benchmark Books, 2003.

Gregory, Kristiana. *Seeds of Hope: The Gold Rush Diary of Susanna Fairchild, California Territory, 1849*. New York: Scholastic, 2001.

Hatch, Linda. *California Gold Rush Trail*. New York: McGraw-Hill Children's Publishing, 1996.

Ito, Tom. *The California Gold Rush*. San Diego, Calif.: Lucent Books, 1998.

Kallen, Stuart A. *A Travel Guide to California Gold Country*. San Diego, Calif.: Lucent Books, 2003.

Ketchum, Liza. *The Gold Rush*. Boston: Little, Brown and Co., 1996.

Lloyd, J. D. *Gold Rush*. Farmington Hills, Mich.: Thomson Gale, 2002.

Rawls, Jim. *Dame Shirley and the Gold Rush*. Orlando: Steck-Vaughn, 1993.

Saffer, Barbara. *The California Gold Rush*. Broomall, Pa.: Mason Crest Publishers, 2003.

Stanley, Jerry. *Hurry Freedom: African Americans in Gold Rush California*. New York: Crown Publishers, 2000.

Uschan, Michael V. *The California Gold Rush*. Milwaukee, Wis.: World Almanac Library, 2003.